THE
FRIDAY
EMAIL

THE FRIDAY EMAIL

88 TIPS
FOR
ASPIRING
LEADERS

RENÉE MCGOWAN

World Scientific

NEW JERSEY · LONDON · SINGAPORE · BEIJING · SHANGHAI · HONG KONG · TAIPEI · CHENNAI · TOKYO

Published by

World Scientific Publishing Co. Pte. Ltd.

5 Toh Tuck Link, Singapore 596224

USA office: 27 Warren Street, Suite 401-402, Hackensack, NJ 07601

UK office: 57 Shelton Street, Covent Garden, London WC2H 9HE

Library of Congress Cataloging-in-Publication Data

Names: McGowan, Renée, author.

Title: The Friday email : 88 tips for aspiring leaders / Renée McGowan.

Description: New Jersey : World Scientific, [2024] | Includes bibliographical references.

Identifiers: LCCN 2023046429 | ISBN 9789811284663 (hardcover) |
    ISBN 9789811284977 (paperback) | ISBN 9789811284670 (ebook)

Subjects: LCSH: Leadership.

Classification: LCC HD57.7 .M395596 2024 | DDC 658.4/092--dc23/eng/20231005

LC record available at https://lccn.loc.gov/2023046429

British Library Cataloguing-in-Publication Data

A catalogue record for this book is available from the British Library.

For any available supplementary material, please visit
https://www.worldscientific.com/worldscibooks/10.1142/13634#t=suppl

Desk Editor: Claire Lum

Editor: Low Shi Ping

CONTENTS

Why I Have Written This Book

"If you could write a book about your life, what would the title be and why?" This was one of many rapid-fire, thought-provoking questions posed to me in an all-colleague meeting.

While I wish I could have thought of something as inspiring as Michelle Obama's *Becoming*, the title of my book would be much closer to *Work In Progress*. I am a woman, a mother, a business leader and a lifelong learner. Above all else, I am still very much a "work in progress".

Why then, you might wonder, would someone who feels she still has unfinished business be compelled to write a book? For starters, this book is not about my life. Rather, it was born out of a desire to share some (hopefully helpful) insights and inspiration that have supported me on my leadership journey.

Like many, I love to read and have been inspired by the work of many great authors and scholars on the topic of human behaviour, business and leadership. Many of the leading minds – Jim Collins, Liz Wiseman, Carol Dweck – are referenced in this book. But I am frequently short on reading time and increasingly look for the bite-sized nuggets of information that may fuel better decisions or inspire better leadership.

In 2020, as the global pandemic closed borders and offices, I started a dialogue with the more than 2,000 colleagues across 10 markets in Asia in my capacity as the CEO of Asia for Mercer. Delivered via email each Friday, it tried to provide a short business update, some inspiration for the moment and some humanity and empathy for what we were all experiencing and living through.

I was surprised and delighted when colleagues reached out after each email to engage, provide feedback, connect, debate and discuss. These personalised notes, and the positive exchange they generated, are the origins of this book, *The Friday Email*.

Eighty-eight of these emails have been collated into this book, inevitably becoming a mirror of my time leading a multi-national business in Asia. Grouped around eight themes in a nod to the lucky number in Chinese culture, and guided by pillars that embody leadership for me – Purpose, People, Path and Progress – they have been edited to become tips that can be read in one sitting or consumed in bite-sized chunks.

This is not a "how-to" and it does not provide any researched path to leadership success. It is a book that reflects on the topics relevant to all leaders and perhaps to anyone working in our increasingly fast-paced and dynamic world. Each of the 88 tips is written by me – someone who is a "work in progress", in the midst of actually being a leader, through perhaps one of the most challenging times in modern history.

I hope that you keep the book handy. It need not be read sequentially and is best used on those days when you're questioning your abilities, resilience, next move or simply need some inspiration or new ideas. Most importantly, it is here to tell you that you are not alone in what you are feeling.

PURPOSE

GROWTH
AND GRIT ✉

The Asia CEO Update: Are you an everyday leader?

 ⊗ **McGowan, Renee**
To:

Friday, 24 July 2020 at 9:00 AM

Hi everyone,

I hope your week was fabulous. I really enjoyed hearing from so many of you via our Asia Town Hall questions and your feedback after the event. I really appreciated that there were so many thoughtful and challenging questions – thank you. For those who you missed it, you can catch the replay here.

Despite the challenges the world and our business are facing, one of the reasons I'm optimistic about our future is each and every one of you. In the midst of the crisis, I've seen all of you – at all levels – step up, displaying great leadership every day in your own quiet ways. Some of you might be familiar with Drew Dudley's TED Talk on Everyday Leadership, but it resonates today more powerfully than ever. Many of us grow up associating leadership with grand titles and extraordinary deeds that change the world, but leadership at its core can be as simple as the things we do daily to make someone's day a little *brighter*.

It could be helping our teammates make some progress every single day. It may be thoughtful feedback, a helping hand, a quiet pat on the back or a pick-me-up when things are not going their way. It's these little moments that can impact those around us in big ways – often without us even realizing it. For people managers, this calls us to reconsider what leadership means. As MMC CEO Dan Glaser pointed out in his recent video message, people managers are among the most essential people in the company with a huge role in shaping company culture.

Leadership isn't about what we've achieved in the past, but what we do every single day to help and inspire others, be courageous, and impact change. All of us have a choice and chance to be a leader every day. That's really powerful and we need to do more to acknowledge and recognize these moments of leadership. If someone's made your day better, reach out and let them know.

Personally, I've decided to make tomorrow a 'gratitude day'. This year, there have been so many friends and colleagues whom I haven't checked in with or thanked for specific things they've done. After a very long week of hard days and very late night meetings, I'm going to spend a lot of tomorrow reconnecting with colleagues, clients and friends to let them how thankful I am for them in my life. I can't wait and it's something I want to do more of.

This month, we'll launch *Somebuddy Cares*, a buddy program in Asia to help colleagues feel less alone, remind everyone of the available resources and connect people to different parts of the business. As part of our Brighter Together wellness initiative, this is one of many ways we can all support one another and be an everyday leader. I hope to see many of you participate in the program.

Thank you for stepping up every day to our commitments to our clients, our colleagues and communities. Thank you for inspiring me with your daily acts of leadership.

Take care, stay well and feel free to reach out always to me or the Asia Leadership team. We're always up for a cup of virtual coffee (or a drink of any type as you can see from our virtual Happy Hour last night).

Renee

Bill's iPhone

Set great expectations

A t the start of every year, many of us like to spend time reflecting on what we have achieved relative to our goals – what we have done well and what might have been done better. At the same time, we indulge in some form of future-gazing to map out our priorities and action plan for the year.

Setting goals can be as challenging as meeting them. But one of the things I encourage everyone to do is go big and bold. In his book, *The Culture Code*, journalist Daniel Coyle examined the DNA of some of the world's most successful organisations and found that when leaders set a high bar, their people, more often than not, rise to the occasion. An experiment by a team of psychologists, he shares, also showed that a simple phrase, "*I have high expectations and I know you can meet them*", increased the effort of students by 40 percent.

In my career, I have seen this happen time and again. I have had great mentors who believed in me. I remember my first mentor, Annette King, would often leave small notes in my office, usually along the lines of, "I know you're finding it challenging, but you're a star!" I am not sure that I was a star in that particular role, but her high expectations and overt confidence certainly helped me grow and thrive. As a people manager myself, I have also witnessed how people and teams have overcome great odds and thrived when I share the same confidence and belief in them.

Have healthy
ambition

Decades of research have proven that people are likely to rise or fall to the level of our expectations. But this is not just about setting the bar high. It is also about being clear, specific and transparent, so there is no disconnect. And where organisations and teams have been most successful, it is because their managers made every effort to grow their team's capability by supporting and coaching them over the bar.

Having expectations, I believe, is about helping people fulfil their potential. And the same applies to us. Our expectations of ourselves not only set our course but act as a compelling compass towards our goals. It's only when we think big that we realise what we are truly capable of.

TIP #1

Where organisations and teams have been successful, it is because they were backed by strong leadership supporting and coaching them over the bar.

Have healthy ambition

The word "ambitious" can sometimes have a negative connotation. It is often linked with being too assertive or even aggressive, especially when applied to a woman. We get disparaged for a lack of ambition and are frowned upon for being too ambitious. While these misperceptions are deeply rooted in traditional gender roles and unconscious biases (which frankly deserves a whole book on its own), the fact remains that having ambition is good and important.

To have ambition is to know where you are going and what you have to do to get there. It starts with understanding your aspirations and setting goals that have the right level of difficulty and discomfort. Too great of a challenge may leave you discouraged; too little and you risk disinterest. Without the desire to grow and become better, we risk slipping into inertia, becoming bored and never realising our full potential. While ambition, if left unchecked, may backfire, executive coach and author Ron Carucci shares that a healthy level of ambition leads to creativity and innovation, greater levels of performance, and deeper levels of joy and satisfaction at work.

To cultivate healthy ambition, we need to strike a balance between three dimensions:

1. **Performance** (what greater results do I want to achieve for myself and my organisation?);

2. **Growth** (what new levels of technical and skills mastery do I want to achieve?); and

3. **Achievement** (what rewards do I hope to gain from my effort?).

These interplay to provide impetus for development and motivation when the going gets tough.

I love seeing this applied when offering a new role to a team member. I have a general belief that if an individual has 70 to 80 percent of the skills, experiences or qualifications for the role, then with the right support, they can be successful. In this circumstance, when I offer someone a job, I normally ask if the successful candidate feels uncomfortable. Invariably, the answer is yes, and then I can assert, "This is the right role for you". Initial discomfort is almost always overcome through ambition and support.

TIP #2

To have ambition is to know where you are going and what you have to do to get there. Without it, we risk slipping into inertia, becoming bored and never realising our full potential.

Be a goal-getter

Have you ever felt like you are running but not really going anywhere? In the early stages of my career, I was often focused on my to-dos in the present – completing tasks, checking things off lists, accomplishing my deliverables.

It took me some time to realise that my to-do list was frequently full of "urgent" but unimportant tasks. The "urgent" activities kept me very busy, but not necessarily productive. Worse, they eroded the time that should have been spent on thinking about and doing what was most important and impactful.

While addressing our current challenges is important, author and coach Peter Bergman likens it to running on a treadmill – we are running but not really going anywhere. Being busy, he adds, is not the same as being productive. Even when there are more important things to do in the present, we need to create space to focus on our future – to run towards a destination.

Whether it is in our personal or work life, goal-setting provides an opportunity to focus on how we want to spend our time to achieve what we want. And goals work best when they serve a broader purpose. Purpose is a compass, and goals are the actions we take to move in the right direction.

If it is difficult to get started, then break it down: what does success look like? What will I have learnt, achieved, contributed? We can all take small steps to greatness.

TIP #3

Being busy is not the same as being productive. We need to create space to focus on our future – to run towards a destination using deliberate goals.

Think impossible

Growth is the goal of nearly every company. No matter the size, age or industry, small companies want to get big and big companies want to get bigger. But in chasing growth and in discussing strategy, competition and leadership, we tend to get mired in the practical – revenue, costs and resources.

While all that is important, what is critical, I think, is challenging how we think about what is possible. A *Harvard Business Review* article[1] by the co-founder of *Fast Company*, Bill Taylor, highlights the legacy of Roger Bannister, the first human to run a four-minute mile. In conquering what was thought to be unreachable, he gave everyone a new benchmark, something they could now shoot for. In a nutshell, he showed everyone what was possible.

As Taylor puts it, "Great leaders don't just out-perform their rivals. They transform the sense of what's possible in their fields." To unlock our growth potential, we need to think beyond our achievements and defy our limiting thoughts, feelings and beliefs. Our mindsets and deeply ingrained assumptions are what stop us from creating what was not there before.

---

[1] Taylor, Bill. "What Breaking the 4-Minute Mile Taught Us About the Limits of Conventional Thinking." *Harvard Business Review*, 2 December 2021, https://hbr.org/2018/03/what-breaking-the-4-minute-mile-taught-us-about-the-limits-of-conventional-thinking.

I once set a goal for a team I led to double our business in three years. Despite the achievement of good historical growth, this was a lofty ambition. For those who were mathematically inclined, they quickly highlighted the gap between my ambition and the team's past performance. But for me, this was an opportunity to think differently about the future, think beyond past performance and explore what was possible. When we did reach our goal and more, we learnt that the seemingly impossible could be possible.

TIP #4

Unlock growth potential by defying limiting thoughts, feelings and beliefs and aspire to do things that haven't been done before.

To me, leadership is as much about doing things right and doing the right things, as it is about doing things that have not been done before. It is easier said than done. But as Norman Vincent Peale once said, "Shoot for the moon. Even if you miss, you'll land among the stars."

Be an impact player

All of us want purpose in our lives – and that includes at work. We want our work to matter and to make a positive difference in the world. In her bestseller *Impact Players: How to Take the Lead, Play Bigger, and Multiply Your Impact*, Liz Wiseman dissects how we can all make a bigger impact simply by changing how we think and act.

In her research, Wiseman, who defines impact players as standout contributors who bring extraordinary value whenever they work, found that they share a few key traits. They do not just do their job but are constantly figuring out what is important to their business and do what is needed. Instead of waiting for direction at every turn, they step up and take on the next challenge even before they are asked. Where others see threats, they see opportunity. Instead of simply escalating a complex or unforeseen obstacle, they embrace it as an opportunity to bring value.

At the heart of every impact player is a learning and growth mindset. They are constantly building new skillsets to adapt to change rather than sticking to old playbooks and what they know best.

Through my career, I have learned that success does not lie in a few superstars but in teams of all-stars. We can all become impact players in our areas of responsibilities and work. Here is how:

1. **Stay curious and ask great questions** – This helps everyone get to the core of issues, so they can move faster and with greater impact.

2. **Do not wait for direction** – Step up and lead, especially when it is unclear who is in charge. Leadership does not need a title.

3. **Finish strong** – Do what it takes to move things across the finish line especially when others have given up.

TIP #5
At the heart of every impact player is a learning and growth mindset – someone who is constantly building new skillsets to adapt to change, rather than sticking to old playbooks and familiar ways.

Build a reservoir of grit

The rapid shift in leadership that the pandemic necessitated convinced me that tomorrow's leaders will need to be very different. Tomorrow's leaders will be defined not just by their business acumen and decision-making, but also by their personal grit, transparency, empathy and agility.

The pandemic called on all of us to dig deep into our reservoirs of grit. Personally, I had to dig *really* deep. As a leader, it was both hard and draining to be feeling the same uncertainty, concern and fear as everyone else, but also to absorb their emotions and try to move forward with (realistic) positivity. What I learnt is that for me, grit is about resilience, about suffering setbacks and challenges – and getting back up. It is setting your mind to do something and sticking with it – no matter what comes our way. It is perhaps best summed up by the phrase "when the going gets tough, the tough get going". I try to take a positive outlook fuelled by grit and resilience into the still-volatile, post-pandemic world.

Undoubtedly, when things go wrong, it can be easy to despair. In his book *Buddha's Brain*, neuroscientist Rick Hanson likens our brain to Velcro for negative experiences and Teflon for positive ones. As humans, we are hardwired to focus on the bad instead of the good. We overestimate obstacles but underestimate our ability to

Create your pocket
of greatness

overcome them. It is also why we agonise over our wrong answers and forget the ones we got right.

As a young, opinionated new manager, I often voiced my disagreement (don't get me wrong, being vocal is good) whenever I did not see eye-to-eye with my then-boss-now-mentor, David Anderson. One day, he pulled me aside and helped me see that we all view the world through our own frame of reference.

TIP #6

By harnessing the power of slower, reflective thought, we can turn helplessness to grit and embrace failure as a necessary part of success.

What I had failed to see are the broader frames of references that others might have based on their personal knowledge or experiences. Today, instead of knee-jerk disagreement, I stop to pause, reflect and ask myself if I have the full context. By harnessing the power of slower, reflective thought, we can turn helplessness to grit and embrace failure as a necessary part of success. By broadening our frames of reference, you will see that there are more possibilities and often find better solutions.

Create your pocket of greatness

I f you could write a book about your life, what would be the title and why? That was one of many rapid-fire questions posed to me at an all-colleague meeting and also one of the most thought-provoking.

My answer then (with a laugh) was, "I wish I could think of something as inspiring as Michelle Obama's *Becoming*, but the title of my book would be much closer to *Work in Progress*."

In hindsight, my on-the-spot response is not far from the truth. Greatness, as Jim Collins, author of *Good to Great*, puts it, is not a moment or an epiphany. Companies that achieve greatness never see themselves as great, but just on a journey to get better and better. The same goes for us. It is also why I love Carol Dweck's idea of a growth mindset. For me, a growth mindset is all about always trying to become a better version of myself.

Our success can only be possible when each of us is empowered and committed to be the best at what we do. In his book, Collins also highlights that when each of us takes responsibility for our own area of work and influence to make great what we can make great, we can all create a pocket of greatness.

I try to do this often, relentlessly prioritising what I do best and, at the same time, relentlessly learning what I need to know. It does not matter who you are or where you are in your career; every one of us has the power to be the best at our craft and make a meaningful difference. Recognising we are all a work in progress is a good first step into greatness.

TIP #7

It does not matter who or where you are in life or your career; every one of us has the power to be the best at what we do and make a meaningful difference.

Choose mastery over success

My family and I are fans of the Olympics. We love rooting for our country, favourite teams and athletes. We love how it brings the world together to celebrate the best of sportsmanship and the human spirit. But most of all, we love the many inspiring stories of resilience, talent and determination that emerge from the games. While not all athletes walk away with the gold medal they came for, they all deserve a medal for grit, perseverance and defying the odds to make it to the Games.

As someone who is not particularly athletic, I have always been curious about what propels these athletes in their constant pursuit of excellence. In her TED Talk, art historian and the author of *The Rise: Creativity, the Gift of Failure, and the Search for Mastery*, Sarah Lewis, makes a distinction between success and mastery.

Success, she says, is a moment in time, but mastery is in the reaching, not the arriving. It is about constantly wanting to close the gap between where we are today and where we want to be. What propels us forward are these gaps – the near-wins on our journey. In her words, "We thrive not when we've done it all, but when we still have more to do."

That certainly rings true for me. In my own life and my professional career, I have found that success is satisfying, but mastery is the most rewarding. Few of us ever get anything right the first time – skill and mastery takes practice. And as we strive to get better at what we do, it is these "near-wins" that push us to continue to grow and improve. Rather than view these near-wins as failures, we need to use them as fuel that keeps us going.

TIP #8

Mastery is in the reaching, not the arriving. It is about constantly wanting to close the gap – the "near-wins" on our journey – between where we are today and where we want to be.

Cultivate an abundance mindset

Growing up, my sister and I were not allowed to say, "I can't." Our Dad would always correct us, "Don't say 'I can't', just say: 'I'll try', 'I'm learning' or 'I can do part of that'." It was simultaneously frustrating and encouraging at the same time; but with hindsight, it was a powerful lifelong lesson that I have reflected on often when faced with daunting tasks or options.

Dad probably did not know it then, but he was echoing the late Stephen Covey's idea of an abundance mindset. This, Covey says, shifts your thinking from "I can't" to "How can I?", and "Not enough" to "There's always more – how can we make that happen?". It comes with focusing on what we have in the present and training your mind to recognise the possibilities.

In stark contrast, a scarcity mindset hurts us all. A term first coined also by Covey in his best-seller *The 7 Habits of Highly Effective People*, the scarcity mindset, simply put, is seeing life as a finite pie – some get larger slices, which leaves less for others. This constant fear of "not enough" breeds competition instead of col-

Nurture Intentional growth

laboration, focuses on problems instead of possibilities and emphasises limitations instead of the opportunities that come with what we have on hand. Being narrowly focused on what we do not have erodes our capacity to make choices and see fresh possibilities.

I am a firm believer that we become what we think. Early on in my career, I exhibited this scarcity mindset; I used to think that to win, someone had to lose. Thankfully one of my great mentors, Ben Walsh, pulled me aside and said "for me to succeed, they need to succeed". It was a learning moment that, for me, was a gamechanger in my leadership journey.

TIP #9

An abundance mindset shifts your thinking from "I can't" to "How can I?", and "Not enough" to "There's always more – how can we make that happen?".

Nurture intentional growth

A question I like to ask myself – and should do so more often – is how much have I grown and in what areas can I continue to grow? This is a question I encourage everyone to ask themselves.

Early on in my career, I learnt that growth does not just happen. As leadership guru John Maxwell puts it, "If you're going to grow, the only way to do so is if you're intentional about it. Not only do we need a roadmap for where we want to be, we need to invest continually in ourselves and constantly seek to move out of our comfort zone ("I do what I already know I can") to a challenge zone ("I attempt to do what I haven't done before")."

Just as important is immersing ourselves in a growth environment. In his bestseller *The Leadership Handbook*, Maxwell paints what a growth environment looks like. It is one where you are continually challenged; where the focus is forward (on the future and not past mistakes) and where the atmosphere is affirming, with people spurring one another on to do better.

But driving growth is not always easy. As Tony Schwartz, CEO of The Energy Project, shares[1], in his company's shift from a culture focused on performance to one focused on growth, a performance culture can lean toward zero-sum gain where there are winners and losers in an organisation.

A growth culture, however, requires an environment of safety, learning, experimentation and continuous feedback. By definition, in a growth culture, we must view and embrace failure, both as an organisation and individual, as a way to learn, not lose. And this is the environment we should all aim to create in every team and organisation that we manage.

TIP #10

We need to invest continually in ourselves and constantly seek to move out of our comfort zone ("I do what I already know I can") to a challenge zone ("I attempt to do what I haven't done before").

[1] Schwartz, Tony. "Create a Growth Culture, Not a Performance-Obsessed One." *Harvard Business Review*, 3 June 2021, https://hbr.org/2018/03/create-a-growth-culture-not-a-performance-obsessed-one.

Define your future self

"**W**here do you see yourself in five or 10 years?" This is a common question asked by potential employers with no lack of sample answers on the Internet. While many of us may brush this off with a generic response around our career aspirations and goals around our personal and professional development, I think our response merits greater attention.

Defining our future self is critical for growth. What we do, how we act and what we choose to invest in today is shaped by our view of our future. And we can start by simply asking, "Who do I want to be? Where do I want to go?"

For me, this is not about defining what roles I want to have and where. Rather, it is defining who I want to be at points in my life and career and how I want this to change over time. I knew, for example, that I wanted to spend much of my time with my children while they were young, and so I worked part-time for about eight years. Later, I knew that I wanted to have more challenging roles and explore opportunities overseas, and so I defined at what point in my life and career that made sense.

In his TED Talk, Harvard psychologist Dan Gilbert points out interestingly that most of us often think that the person we are right now is the person we will be for the rest of our lives. A study he conducted found that at every age, from 18 to 68, people vastly under-estimate how much change they would experience over the next decade. That is because it is always easier – and more comfortable – to default to the present than to imagine a different future.

Defining our future self is also a big part of having a growth mindset, choosing not to be defined by our present, but by who we want to be. The same applies to organisations. What your company invests in today, whether it is expanding the capabilities of your people, new solutions or technology, needs to empower your future enterprise. It is a delicate balancing act – tackling your challenges of the day while being on the offense to seize the opportunities tomorrow creates – but one that is well worth the challenge.

TIP #11

Defining our future self is critical for growth. What we do, how we act and what we choose to invest in today is shaped by our view of our future.

Be an every-day leader

Many of us grow up associating leadership with grand titles and extraordinary deeds that change the world. Yet, leadership at its core can be as simple as the things we do daily to make someone's day a little brighter.

It could be helping our teammates make some progress every single day. It could be thoughtful feedback, a helping hand, a quiet pat on the back or a pick-me-up when things are not going their way. It is these little moments that can impact those around us in big ways – often without us even realising it. For people managers, this calls us to reconsider what leadership means.

Drew Dudley, in his TED Talk about everyday leadership, says, "As long as we make leadership something bigger than us, as long as we keep leadership beyond us and make it about changing the world, we give ourselves an excuse not to expect it every day, from ourselves and from each other."

Drew's words really resonated with me. In my early career, leadership was BIG – my examples were political and historical leaders of history that changed the world. I wanted to be one of them, until I realised that I was confusing admiring their greatness and aspiring to be them (when it was unlikely I was ever going to be a Winston Churchill or Martin Luther King!).

My closest friend, colleague and mentor Andrew Godfrey, through his own leadership skills, helped me to find a more realistic perspective. Over many years, he both demonstrated and coached me to see the value in small actions with a positive outlook, in taking the time to acknowledge someone's good work and to say thank you. This helped me go back to the basics – how could I show up as a leader every day, in my own way? In addition to more regularly saying thanks, I started setting aside "gratitude days", where I reconnected with colleagues, clients and friends to let them know how thankful I was for them in my life.

TIP #12

Leadership is not about what we have achieved in the past, but what we do every single day to help and inspire others, be courageous and impact change.

Leadership is not about what we have achieved in the past, but what we do every single day to help and inspire others, be courageous and impact change. All of us have a choice and chance to be a leader every day. That is really powerful and we need to do more to acknowledge and recognise these moments of leadership. So if someone has made your day better, make a point to reach out and let them know.

Slow down to go faster

When I think about growth, I cannot help but get excited – and want to go full steam ahead with all that is planned immediately! Growth, for me, is more than just financial performance. It brings more opportunities for colleagues to grow in their careers. It allows us to do more and do better for clients and the communities in which we work, live and play.

However, over many years, I have learnt it is helpful to pause and slow down. Slowing down, I have realised, actually helps to accelerate success. It may sound counter-intuitive, but in today's hyper-fast world, where every instinct tells us to run faster to keep up, taking it slow gives clarity for better decisions and space for more innovation.

Do not get me wrong. I am not saying we should not focus on efficiency or the speed of execution whenever possible. In their *Harvard Business Review* article "Need Speed? Slow Down", Jocelyn R Davis and Tom Atkinson make a distinction between operational speed (moving quickly) with strategic speed (reducing the time it takes to deliver value). They found that firms that embraced initiatives and chose to go, go, go ended up with lower sales and operating profits than those that paused at key moments to make sure they were spending time on the right things and that they were on track.

This may mean that solution roll-outs or new market launches may take longer or may be fewer in number, but getting it right will ultimately reap better results than going at it fast. It may mean being very disciplined in how and when you invest and doing a few things very well to accelerate our growth.

TIP #13

In today's hyper-fast world where every instinct tells us to run faster to keep up, taking it slow gives clarity for better decisions and space for more innovation.

The same applies to our day-to-day life. Often, we rush to react, to tick a checkbox on our to-do list when what we really need to do is slow down, ask the right questions and see the bigger picture. As we aim to run fast, we should also pause to ask if we are running in the right direction.

PURPOSE

FUEL YOUR ENERGY ✉

Hello AMEA: Healthy People, Healthy Organisation

 ⊗ **McGowan, Renee**

To:

Thursday, 15 July 2021 at 9:00 AM

Hi everyone,

I hope you had an awesome week. I returned from my break this week rested, recharged and ready to go. It was invigorating spending quality time with my family, doing activities like scuba diving and catching up on reading. With some planning, I was also glad to be able to unplug and step away from my devices and screens. Powering down really gave me an opportunity to recover, reset and refocus my mind.

During my holidays, I read _The Advantage_ by management expert Patrick Lencioni, a book Martine kindly gave to me. Centered on healthy organisations, Lencioni asserts that organisations succeed not because of smart strategy, marketing, finance or technology – these are all a given. Rather, successful organisations are characterised by a more subjective fitness – where politics and confusion are minimised; morale and productivity are high; and there is reasonable turnover.

I agree with Lencioni on these requirements for success, but I also think there is another important element to this – healthy organisations require heathy people. As individuals, we can only contribute our best when we feel at our best. When we are physically and mentally fit, when we have alignment of work and purpose and when we embrace a confident growth mindset, we don't hold ourselves back.

Taking good care of yourself – and caring for others in your team and around you – I believe, is the foundation for a healthy, thriving organisation.

And I hope that in this COVID-19 marathon, all of you are taking time to recharge and reset. I also encourage all of you to complete the Pulse survey which just went out this week, so we can know how better to support you.

In the meantime, have a great weekend and to all of you celebrating Eid al-Adha next week, enjoy the festivities!

Renée

Diving literally into a new adventure!

Be kind to yourself

Some days are harder than others. We miss a deadline. We fail to clinch a deal. We fall sick. We feel like we are falling behind – in our career, our life, everything. On these days, we have to remind ourselves that it's perfectly okay not to be okay – that in the pursuit of our life's purpose, being kind to ourselves is just as important as being kind to others.

Research concurs that one of the best ways to deal with stress, worry, and uncertainty in our life is to practise more deliberate kindness and self-compassion. When we affirm ourselves or look beyond the moment of challenge toward the bigger picture, it forces us to focus on what we can control, not what we cannot.

I used to spend a lot of time focused on what I cannot control and playing out all types of scenarios in my head. Personally, I think women tend to do this more than men. In my case, when offered a new job I would spend more time listing out the reasons why I could not do it – not sufficiently qualified, not the right time for my family, too much travel involved. It took me a long time (and a lot of wasted energy!) to realise how much time I was spending focused on the reasons why I could not – and how little time I was spending on the reasons why I could. Focusing on what I could not control was literally stressing me out about nothing.

So, I have learnt that it is okay to be kind to myself – and in fact it is a necessity. This can take many forms and shapes. A few that work for me are:

1. **Get moving** – This could be running, doing yoga or dancing to your favourite tunes.

   TIP #14
   When we have a positive attitude towards the big picture, it forces us to focus on what we can control, not what we cannot.

2. **Get a good night's rest** – Getting good sleep is essential for health, even more so now. If you find sleep hard to come by, try meditation, reading an inspirational book or putting on your favourite relaxation track. I have found that picking up printed versions of books to read works for me. It gets me offline and engrossed in something completely different. One book I really enjoyed recently was *And the Mountains Echoed* by Khaled Hosseini.

3. **Give to others** – Doing good can also do you good. This might be a small act of kindness for a family member or friend or finding a way to give back in your community.

Practise gratitude

Thanksgiving is a lovely American tradition that I have adopted after living in New York. It is not just because I love the togetherness, food and occasion, but I also appreciate the reminder to explicitly give thanks for all that I am grateful for. It is a kindness that benefits everyone and I am sure we would all reap the rewards of giving thanks frequently, not just once a year.

Research shows a strong association between gratitude and greater happiness. People who consciously count their blessings experience more positive emotions, improve their health, deal with adversity better and build stronger relationships.

At Thanksgiving each year, my family and I complete the tradition of moving around the table and listing what we are grateful for. We usually have guests with us and while it is a little awkward to start, we all soon get into the spirit of gratitude, and it is uplifting.

I encourage everyone to find time to acknowledge the goodness in their lives and to do it often. Here is my list:

1. **Education and Learning** – I am forever grateful for the support I received through scholarships and financial aid to further my education. It changed my life. I am equally grateful to be able to continue with lifelong learning, both formally and informally, through experiences living and working with different cultures and colleagues around the world.

2. **Health** – We should be thankful for good health when we have it. But sometimes it is so easy to take good health for granted. My unexpected cancer diagnosis in 2022 (now thankfully all clear) was a much-needed reminder that I need to "invest" in my health proactively and not just deal with health issues reactively.

TIP #15

Find time to acknowledge the good things in your life and do it often.

3. **Family and Friends** – It is a blessing to have the love and support of both family and friends around the world. Distance does not break strong bonds. Whether virtual or in person, they have been supportive, encouraging and caring. I am thankful for all I have received from my friends, family (and even medical professionals) and tell them personally.

4. **Work** – My work is a privilege and I love it. The work I have done at Mercer and Marsh McLennan positively impacts thousands of organisations and improves the lives of millions. Additionally, I get to do this work with colleagues all around the world that are intelligent, funny, caring and inspiring, and I tell them this as much as I can.

Define your fears

No matter how seasoned a leader we are, we are bound to have moments of stress, anxiety and even self-doubt. Often, our heads conjure up the worst possible outcomes and scenarios and we tell ourselves all kinds of anxious stories about the future.

This is true for me, especially in the first three months of any new role that I take on. In those early months when I am inundated with new information and challenged by new issues, I initially always think "I've bitten off more than I can chew". Inevitably, mistakes are made or misunderstandings occur and it does not take long for anxious self-doubt to bubble up. In the moment, I lack the clarity to reason that what I am experiencing is probably a typical and appropriate response to a challenging new job – and the situation and role will become more manageable over time.

In his TED Talk, American entrepreneur and lifestyle guru Tim Ferriss discusses the importance of defining our fears, a practice he uses to overcome self-paralysis and thrive in high-stress environments. While fear is sometimes justified, they are, more often than not, phantoms that lurk in the crevices of our minds. By defining – and writing down – our fears, we shine a light on them and find out that they are usually not as bad as we have imagined. The more specific we get with our fears, the more manageable they become.

Ferriss calls this fear-setting. You define your fears by writing down all the worst things you can imagine happening. Then, in another column, write down everything you can do to prevent all of it from happening. Lastly, write down what you can do to repair the situation should your worst fears come through.

TIP #16
By articulating our fears, we shine a light on them and find out that they are usually not as bad as we have imagined.

I have found this really helpful as a way to objectively think through what I am feeling and thinking. And often times, it has proven, as the ancient Roman philosopher Seneca puts it, "We suffer more often in imagination than in reality."

Nurture self-compassion

Many of you may be familiar with Christine Ha. Known as the first blind contestant who went on to win MasterChef America's third season, the Houston-based chef thought her life was over when she lost her eyesight to a rare auto-immune disease. But as it turned out, it was just the beginning.

Today, Christine is an accomplished cookbook author, owner of two restaurants The Blind Goat and Xin Chào (opened during the pandemic!) and continues to impact lives through her inspiring story.

I had the privilege of hosting a fireside chat with Christine at an internal Mercer event in 2022. While her courage and resilience in relearning how to live and cook as she gradually lost her vision from the age of 20 was uplifting, what really hit home were her thoughts on self-compassion.

In high-achieving cultures, many of us tend to drive ourselves hard. In our constant push for perfection, we criticise ourselves more harshly than we should for our mistakes and failures. Self-compassion does not mean avoiding responsibility for things that have gone wrong; rather it is acknowledging challenges and mistakes and giving yourself space and grace to learn from them.

As she gradually lost her sight, Christine had to relearn cooking over and over again. Through it, she realised that taking on a new challenge is never going to be easy and we will fail – often more than once. But it is by keeping at it over and over again, and

Shift away from
being "always on"

accepting mistakes as part of learning, while being kind to ourselves, that we will see progress.

As a leader, I find that while I understand the benefits of self-compassion, we often hesitate to practice it. The reason is simple: we believe we need to be hard on ourselves in order to motivate ourselves. However, research shows that the opposite is true: being kind to ourselves empowers us to grow and give.

My kids often remind me of this. As teenagers, they are all mostly relaxed, happy and big fans of "just hanging out". While I will have a long list of things I want to do with them each weekend, they will have a shorter (or non-existent) list that mostly involves friends, a little bit of family and a lot of "just hanging out".

I tend to create an action-packed weekend list, and then feel bad or like I am wasting a weekend if I do not complete it. My kids often ground me. If I am tired, they remind me that I have worked hard all week; that we probably did not spend as much time together as we would like; and that "chilling" at home with take-out and a movie is a good weekend.

They are right, but still, I do struggle to naturally find this self-compassion to rest.

TIP #17
Self-compassion does not mean avoiding responsibility; rather it is acknowledging challenges and giving yourself space and grace to learn from them.

Shift away from being "always on"

Much of the conversation around the future of work has been focused around where we will work when in fact, we should be spending more time focusing on how we will work. That, I believe, will have the most profound impact on both work and our lives.

A podcast, in which Ezra Klein from *The New York Times* interviewed Cal Newport – author of *A World Without Email* – about the way we work and the destructive nature of constant interruption and required responsiveness, was particularly illuminating[1]. Technology has transformed the way we work in unimaginable ways. The introduction of email – and then real-time collaboration tools such as Teams and Slack – make it easy to ask, respond and resolve. Newport describes this as the hyperactive hive mind, defined as "a workflow centred on ongoing conversation fuelled by unstructured and unscheduled messages".

The world is increasingly working in this mode, relying on ad-hoc, unscheduled digital conversations as our main mode of collaboration and resolving issues on the fly. Our measure of productivity has inadvertently become linked to responsiveness, when in reality, this urge to constantly respond is limiting our productivity. It has impacted not just our focus on the bigger issues,

---

[1] Klein, Ezra, host. "Stop. Breathe. We Can't Keep Working Like This." *The Ezra Klein Show*, The New York Times, 5 March 2021. https://www.nytimes.com/2021/03/05/opinion/ezra-klein-podcast-cal-newport.html.

but also our sense of well-being both at work and at home. Newport argues that this is not the way to go and companies need to seriously rethink work for the digital age. I could not agree more.

But changing how we work, he points out, does not happen overnight. While we are all familiar with how Henry Ford pioneered the car assembly line, not many know the years of trial, error, experimentation and costs it took to create this new way of work. I am hopeful that all the focus on "the future of work" will accelerate positive change in the way we work – to consider how we can work in more structured ways that minimise the deluge of digital back-and-forth, and how we use technology as a considered tool in the workplace and move away from the need to be "always on".

TIP #18

Our measure of productivity has inadvertently become linked to responsiveness, but this urge to constantly respond is limiting our productivity.

Ditching our inboxes entirely may not be possible immediately, but making adjustments to our work habits is definitely doable. It can be as simple as being more thoughtful about emails that we send or implementing processes (e.g. blocking time to do deep work) to regain control of our workflow. After all, technology should support – and not distract us from – what we want to accomplish.

Subtract to add

Achieving balance – or the right type of integration – between work and our life priorities is important but challenging. With work, family, kids, marriage, friends and health constantly jockeying for our attention and energy, I always find taking a break and being in a different environment rejuvenating.

It gives me an opportunity to slow down a little, rush less, pause and think more. A valuable lesson I have learnt is that progress and success is not always about doing more and taking on everything that comes our way. It took me too many years (and some painful moments) to learn that you cannot just run harder, or work more.

Our human instinct is to add. We make to-do, not not-to-do lists. We add words when we try to improve a memo. We default to new initiatives or processes to fix challenges. While there is nothing fundamentally wrong with adding, not considering what we can subtract to solve a problem could mean we are missing out. As the

Harvard Business Review authors Gabrielle Adams, Benjamin A Converse, Andrew Hales and Leidy Klotz write, it could be forfeiting "a whole class of other opportunities"[1] – whether it is getting rid of unnecessary words to make a pitch stronger or removing features from an app to make it simpler to navigate.

Adding and subtracting are not a case of either-or. But when we consider what to add as much as what to leave out, we could come up with innovative ideas that make a bigger impact with less.

TIP #19

There is nothing fundamentally wrong with adding, but not considering what we can subtract could mean we are missing out on other opportunities.

---

[1] Adams, Gabrielle et al. "When Subtraction Adds Value." *Harvard Business Review*, 4 February 2022, https://hbr.org/2022/02/when-subtraction-adds-value.

Make time for down time

I n our 24/7 world, it can be hard to make space for downtime. But just as it is healthy to focus at work, it is just as essential that we find time to refill our cup.

From having brief breaks during the course of the work day, to taking extended time-off, there is plenty of research that shows that downtime can be beneficial. Putting our heads down and bulldozing through our to-do lists, thinking we have little time for days off, free evenings or a weekend break, more often than not leaves us less productive and less focused.

This is why I always encourage my teams to make time for down time. Even short breaks have been proven to help us perform at our best. A study conducted by George Mason University found that students who were given breaks (even as short as five minutes) performed better on attention tasks than those who slogged away without one.

And it does not have to take complicated planning. There are simple steps we can all take to thrive and flourish. Assessing and acknowledging how you feel is an important first step. Taking time

Take restorative
breaks

out to celebrate the little wins or creating a weekly gratitude ritual (e.g. Sunday dinner with the family, calling a friend to check on them) can all boost our well-being. Embedding little acts of kindness in our lives or picking up a new hobby can all help us to "punch out" from work and make new connections.

I carve out my family time with discipline – 7pm is when we dine together and no devices are allowed at the table. Breaks, brief or otherwise, always bring me back to a state of what psychologists call "flourishing", a sense of fulfilment, purpose and happiness. If you have been feeling "meh" recently, and cannot quite put your finger on why, a break might be just what you need.

TIP #20

Continually bulldozing through to-do lists, thinking we have little time for days off, free evenings or a weekend break more often than not leaves us less productive and less focused.

Take restorative breaks

Much has been said about the importance of taking breaks. But I love Daniel Pink's take on it. The author of *WHEN: The Scientific Secrets of Perfect Timing* says we should embrace breaks as part of our performance and not a deviation from it. Time and again, research shows that we are more productive, more replenished, more creative, happier and do better in our jobs if we take more breaks.

Personally, I am up and moving around between each meeting. These include everything from making a cup of coffee to chatting with a colleague for a few minutes. This might possibly be annoying for those who sit around me, but for me, these incidental moments and connections are often the best parts of the day (and as a leader, one of the important ways to get the pulse of the organisation).

The type of breaks we take and how we spend our time during those breaks matter. No, scrolling through your social media feed does not count. To ensure your breaks are replenishing, Dan recommends moving over being stationary (think exercise); taking breaks together with people over going solo and being fully detached.

This means detaching not just your body but also your mind – no talk about work or bringing your phone. He also recommends going outdoors over staying indoors.

The restorative effects of nature on our mind and body – and I can attest to that – are astonishing. When living in Hong Kong, the Mercer Asia CFO and I started a routine of early morning Friday meetings, where we would walk 10km and unpack and upload the week, tie up loose ends and discuss challenges outstanding. It was one of the most productive times of the week for both of us and when we got to the office by mid-morning, we both felt healthy, refreshed and organised.

TIP #21

To ensure your breaks are replenishing, choose moving over being stationary; taking breaks together with people over going solo; being fully detached; and going outdoors over staying indoors.

Plug into nature

I have found that disconnecting from the daily grind from time to time gives me greater mental clarity and boosts my productivity and creativity. One of my favourite ways of refuelling and recharging is to unplug from work and plug into nature through walks and hikes. Dr Zach Bush, whom I have had the pleasure of listening to at a work event, has an interesting view on how nature positively impacts our health and well-being. I was particularly intrigued by Dr Bush's perspective on the importance and connectivity of nature to gut and brain health.

He asserts that the microbiome (bacteria, fungi, viruses) in our gut is directly impacted by our access and engagement with nature (air, soil, water). Protecting our environment, reducing toxicity and engaging with nature improves our gut health, which in turn positively impacts our brain. In one study, his research concluded that 90 percent of serotonin (the neurochemical which impacts our mood, creative capacity, etc.) is actually produced in the gut lining rather than the brain itself. The science around this topic is fascinating.

Other research has shown that connecting with nature helps reduce stress. Studies reveal that spending as little as 10 minutes a day in natural surroundings helps us feel happier and reduces physical and psychological stress, while soaking in a window view of nature from your office can also improve your overall well-being.

So instead of reaching for your phone or a cup of coffee when you need a break or an energy boost, reach for nature.

TIP #22

Spending as little as 10 minutes a day in natural surroundings helps us feel happier and reduces physical and psychological stress.

Be the best version of you

It has been said in sports that the fourth quarter is when games are often won or lost. Coaches – like business leaders – understand the need to finish strong.

Whenever we enter the final quarter of a year, many of us invariably look to sprint to the finish line to achieve our goals or to get as close as we possibly can. It is often a busy and stressful period as we pull out the stops to close deals and strengthen our pipeline for a solid start next year – all the while juggling life and our other commitments. But whether we are on track to hit the mark or have fallen behind, I believe what truly matters is that we are striving to be a better self every day.

In her inspiring TED Talk, Bhakti Sharma, the first Asian woman and youngest in the world to set a record in open swimming in Antarctica, shares how she learned – through her triumphs and tribulations in the waters – that a truly successful life is one spent

Celebrate the small wins

in pursuit of becoming the best version of yourself. One thing she highlighted that resonated deeply with me was that our "best" can change from day to day and it is okay. "Best" on a difficult day could just be not giving up or just completing the tasks that we can.

As leaders, we should high set standards for our teams and also for ourselves. But we should not be too hard on ourselves either. Amid the busyness of life, all we can and should do is be the best we can at any moment in time.

TIP #23

Our "best" can change from day to day and it is okay. "Best" on a difficult day could just be not giving up or just completing the tasks that we can.

Celebrate the small wins

My youngest son Nate and I have a weekly ritual. Every Friday morning, we do a little dance around the house and sing, "It's Fri-yay, Fri-yay, Fri-yay." For Nate, it is about celebrating the end of the school week; for me, it is a weekly reminder that we need to take time to celebrate the "little wins", especially when life and work seem to throw challenges at every turn.

People often save celebrations for their greatest achievements or proudest work moments. At work, awards may only be given to top sales performers. At school, awards tend to celebrate only academic or sporting excellence.

Celebrating achievements is important, but the celebratory moment often overlooks the time, effort, milestones and progress it took to get there. We should celebrate achievements, but we should not overlook the importance of just making progress. Like conquering a summit or completing a masterpiece, it is the many little steps and brushstrokes that build our character and resilience, not the accomplishment itself.

In my interactions with colleagues, I have found that those who are achievement-driven struggle with celebrating wins, downplaying what they have accomplished and move on to the next thing quickly. But it is important not to. The idea of small wins adding up to bigger ones is a theory Professors Teresa Amabile and Steven J Kramer at the Harvard Business School call the Progress Principle. It motivates you to move forward, gives confidence and takes you a step closer to your greater goal.

Celebrating small wins does not have to be complex. It can be as simple as sharing with someone how proud you are of what you have accomplished, giving yourself a small treat or even doing a silly Friday dance. It does not matter how you choose to give yourself a pat on the back, what matters is you do it.

TIP #24

Taking time to celebrate small wins motivates you to move forward, gives confidence and takes you a step closer to your greater goal.

Build healthy organisations with healthy people

One of the most insightful management books I have read is *The Advantage* by management expert Patrick Lencioni. Centred on healthy organisations, it asserts that organisations succeed not because of smart strategy, marketing, finance or technology – these are all a given. Rather, successful ones are characterised by a more subjective fitness – where politics and confusion are minimised; morale and productivity are high; and there is reasonable turnover.

I agree with Lencioni on these requirements for success, but I also think there is another important element to this: healthy organisations require heathy people. As individuals, we can only contribute our best when we feel at our best. When we are physically and mentally fit, when we have alignment of work and purpose and when we embrace a confident growth mindset, we do not hold ourselves back.

In helping organisations address their talent challenges, I have found that top-performing companies go beyond well-being, learning and development programmes. There is a high level of trust, transparency and above all, a sense of belonging and growth. With it comes greater agility, more innovation and an ability to better retain and attract talent.

I have seen this first-hand in some of the best teams I have been in and worked with. When everyone is healthy – as individuals and as a team – there is often a high level of positive energy and a healthy amount of debate, which invariably turns good ideas into better ones. It can also be a lot of fun!

I remember my first "high-performing team". We used to have regular meetings to assess our performance and adjust our strategy. Before long, we realised we had been relegated to the meeting room furthest away from any colleague or client meeting rooms. We were told it was because our meetings were consistently noisy from our debates. It was a proud moment.

TIP #25

When we are physically and mentally fit, when we have alignment of work and purpose and when we embrace a confident growth mindset, we do not hold ourselves back.

As leaders, there is always more we can do to help our companies thrive. For me, it always starts with taking care of people.

PEOPLE

WHEN
EVERYONE
WINS ✉

Hello AMEA: Embracing the New

 ⊚ **McGowan, Renee**
To:

Friday, 12 August 2022 at 10:00 AM

Hi everyone,

I hope you had a great week. Mine was energizing, finalizing our 2023-25 Strategic Plan for AMEA and spending time with some of our new joiners at Mercer.

Did you know that our attrition rate has slowed and that we've welcomed 340 new joiners to the AMEA region this year? This means we have 170 more colleagues than we did this time last year — reflecting our strong growth. We often spotlight our new colleagues in Going Places, our monthly AMEA newsletter, and I know that in many markets, you have formal and informal events to welcome them.

One (of the many) things I love about growth and #goingplacestogether is that we get to create new opportunities for existing colleagues and welcome new ones. Our new colleagues bring with them their own experiences, different perspectives and diverse points-of-view — all things that make us stronger and better as a firm.

I enjoy taking time to meet with our new joiners. Listening to their stories and life experiences, I'm invariably inspired by their diverse backgrounds and always learn something new. In a region as diverse as ours, this usually involves learning more about cultures, customs and different behaviors.

Behavior is learned and it tells others a lot about us as individuals and as a firm. As behavioral scientist Vanessa Van Edwards shares, our behavior — hand gestures, smiles, hello's — not only impacts how others perceive our confidence and ability but is also contagious. This is interesting to me for many reasons, particularly the impact on culture in our organization. How we show up, listen, communicate and support one another can make or break someone else's day. Put simply, we have the opportunity every day to positively "infect" one another with encouraging behaviors.

On that note, I encourage you to reach out to a new colleague this month and introduce yourself. You may not realize it, but your bright smile, confident handshake and enthusiasm go a long way in helping them embrace their new environment.

I'd love to hear how it goes. Have a wonderful weekend!

Renée

Sharing with Team Dubai my NEW experience of harvesting dates from the date palms I discovered in my garden

Get culture right with empathy

From tools that may or may not be helping us to work more efficiently, to solutions to sustain productivity gains, much of the conversation around the future of work and hybrid working has been centred on productivity. While all that is important, I think we are missing the bigger picture – culture.

A lot of research has shown that culture trumps strategy in driving performance. If we get culture right, growth will usually follow. Companies that get culture right, researchers say, excel at supporting and inspiring one another; avoid blame and forgive mistakes; and emphasise the purpose of the work they do. This, in turn, boosts engagement, commitment and well-being.

There are many practical examples of how getting culture right benefits organisations and their employees. Fostering social connections, for example, has been proven to drive positive, healthy cultures. In turn, empirical studies show that people get sick less often, learn faster, display more mental acuity and perform better on the job.

A critical ingredient to getting culture right is empathy. Understanding and sharing the feelings of another person makes a workplace more human and compassionate. From my observation, leaders who exhibit empathy make decisions that have better long-term implications. Such leaders also foster individual and collective resilience – a theme that is critical in today's increasingly volatile and uncertain world.

Additionally, I feel that it is empathy and its associated relational behaviours that make women better leaders, especially in a crisis – and potentially in a world filled with greater ambiguity and volatility. This is increasingly commonly known as "The Female Leadership Advantage".

TIP #26
A magic ingredient for culture is empathy.

I have been fortunate for the past 20 years to work with a company, Mercer, that epitomises a culture of care, open communications and collaboration. During my time in Asia, I had the privilege to work directly for Mercer's then-Global CEO, Martine Ferland, who leads consistently with a balance of empathy and economics. Learning from her has made me a better leader, one who is in turn inspired to make workplaces a kinder, brighter and more positive one for everyone.

Nurture strategy with culture

Many of you may be familiar with the famous quote "culture eats strategy for breakfast", which has sparked many debates over the years about which is more important – culture or strategy.

Proponents of culture say that it is an important differentiator for any company and while anyone can mimic strategy, no one can replicate your culture. No matter how brilliant a strategy is, it will not succeed if people are not inspired or engaged. On the other hand, supporters of strategy argue that no culture, however strong, can overcome poor decisions when it comes to corporate strategy.

In reality, I believe culture and strategy complement and nurture each other. Culture – the behaviours and values we stand for and celebrate – motivates us to do things the right way (the how) and creates the right environment for success. A clear strategy with clear priorities and measurable goals (the what), on the other hand, provides a roadmap for everyone to work in a concerted effort to achieve it.

A great example where culture and strategy have worked hand in hand is at Microsoft, which saw rapid growth when CEO Satya

Nadella came onboard in 2014 and transformed their culture to one of a growth mindset to align with their strategy of innovation. The culture shift at Microsoft boosted employee morale and fuelled its rise as a cloud powerhouse.

This, for me, is a winning combination. Companies should be both performance-driven and, at the same time, values-led. Strategy and culture are inextricably intertwined and reinforce one another. From my experience, the most successful transformations happen when there is a healthy culture in place to support the change, and a clear and realistic strategy that every colleague owns. In short, businesses need both to thrive.

TIP #27

Culture motivates us to do things the right way (the how) and creates the right environment for success. A clear strategy with clear priorities and measurable goals (the what) provides a roadmap for everyone to work in a concerted effort to achieve it.

Make space for play

A s leaders, we all know that a strong company culture is critical to long-term success and cannot be left to chance. But not many have cracked the elusive formula for building a great culture.

One of the most common questions I get is what drives me to do what I do every day. A good, strong cup of coffee aside, what truly gets me going every morning is knowing that what my colleagues and I do make a difference in the lives of many people every day.

In *Primed to Perform: How to Build the Highest Performing Cultures Through the Science of Total Motivation*, authors Lindsay McGregor and Neel Doshi highlight that play, purpose and potential are critical in motivating all of us to be our best at work.

Play, our learning instinct, drives curiosity, experimentation and exploration of challenging problems. **Purpose** connects us with the why behind what we do. We are also more motivated when the work we do enhances our **potential**.

Building a strong culture is about creating an environment where there is room for everyone to innovate and experiment with new ideas and solutions. It is also about helping each colleague see the impact that we make every day, no matter how big or small. And then there is the commitment to help them reach their fullest potential.

To bring this to life, we can start by asking if every employee has space to play and experiment, if they have an opportunity to see the impact of their work and if there are programs in place that can help them fulfil their potential.

TIP #28
Play, purpose and potential are critical in motivating all of us to be our best at work.

A great company culture is not easy to build and does not happen overnight. It takes time and starts by reconnecting with purpose and asking ourselves, "What's our why?" When we connect with our why, the what and how take care of themselves.

Create a safe space

Earlier in my career, I was the type of manager who said "bring me a solution, not the problem" without realising that I was dissuading my team from bringing up problems they found hard to solve or needed support or guidance on. Even if well-intentioned, this approach only makes things worse. Your team will be encouraged to only share the good news while hiding anything that might displease you.

Experience, coupled with the wisdom of great mentors and leaders, has helped me realise that solutions are best created through collaboration. Surfacing problems constructively creates dialogue and encourages ideas. Ideating with others can turn good ideas into great ones. Differences in views, what we do not know or fail to do, are all learning opportunities.

Not every problem will have an easy solution, but it is important that we keep the conversation flowing. It is only when we have different perspectives, backgrounds and experiences that we have new ideas, that we can nip problems in the bud before they become too difficult to manage. But for that to happen, leaders need to nurture an environment where everyone feels safe and encouraged to speak up, share an idea, point out issues, errors or blind spots.

Harvard professor Amy Edmonson, who coined the concept of psychological safety, says, simply put, it is an interpersonal environment where people believe their voice is welcomed, where new ideas and different perspectives are both encouraged and expected. It is about leaders who regularly reach out for and are receptive to feedback. It is about colleagues who feel supported to speak up when they have made mistakes, understanding that failures lead to innovation, not embarrassment.

TIP #29

Surfacing problems constructively creates dialogue and encourages ideas. Ideating with others can turn good ideas into great ones.

Today, one of the first things I do when I manage a new team or take on a new role is to be clear with everyone that it is okay not to know the answer to a problem. Together, we will talk through solutions and collaborate on the next steps. This way, mistakes are out in the open early and setbacks signal learning and an opportunity to build new skills.

Model curiosity

n 2012, Google set out to find what makes the perfect team. An extensive study of 180 Google teams and more than 200 interviews later, researchers found that there were five key characteristics of great teams:

1. **Dependability** – Trust between team members to deliver quality work on time
2. **Structure and clarity** – Everyone is clear about roles, plans and goals
3. **Meaning** – A sense of purpose in their work
4. **Impact** – Belief that their work matters and creates change
5. **Psychological safety** – An environment where team members feel valued, seen and comfortable taking risks

Of these, psychological safety was by far the most important. Google found that colleagues on teams with higher psychological safety were less likely to leave and more likely to harness the power of diverse ideas, bring in greater revenue and were rated more effective.

It is something I have witnessed over the course of my career time and again. I was part of a team some years back, where individual personalities, ages, backgrounds and experiences were all very different. The group genuinely respected one another and the output was high performance and the work was fun!

Conversely, I have sat in meetings where I did not feel confident voicing my opinion or where my opinion, when voiced, was rashly discredited. A workplace where everyone feels safe in being themselves, I have learnt, draws out the best in people, decisions and innovation.

TIP #30

Demonstrating your own curiosity invites the same behaviour, bringing the best in people, decisions and innovation.

To foster psychological safety in a team, I have found that it helps to frame each problem we face as a learning moment. It also helps to be vulnerable and acknowledge that as a leader, you do not have all the answers.

Lastly, ask questions, lots of them. When you model curiosity, you empower your team to share their perspectives, and in the process, discover new possibilities.

Show it is safe
to speak up

There is no doubt that psychologically safe workplaces promote healthier, more productive and more inclusive workforces. They also provide an environment in which innovation can thrive and people can perform at their best.

But they are also rare. Research by Gallup shows that one of the underlying causes of the Great Resignation (a term coined by Anthony Klotz, an associate professor of organisational behaviour at University College of London, to describe the unprecedented rise in the number of workers resigning from their jobs following the pandemic) is the lack of psychological safety.

In trying to create a safe environment, I think it is just as important to understand what psychological safety is not. Psychological safety is not about being nice or always agreeing with one another to keep peace. I have been in one too many meetings when people are polite to one another, only to disagree later when they have private conversations, along with a tendency to dismiss what was agreed at the meeting.

Psychological safety is also not an "anything goes" environment without accountability for high performance standards and deadlines. In workplaces with high psychological safety but low standards, people generally enjoy working with one another but are often not challenged by the work or are particularly productive.

Harvard Professor and author Amy Edmonson, in her book *The Fearless Organisation*, provides numerous examples of how a lack

Regard feedback as a gift

of psychological safety has led to disasters (Volkswagen's Dieselgate, where a culture of fear meant mistakes went unchecked) as well as fearless organisations that have thrived in safe-to-speak-up and safe-to-fail-environments (Google X, for example, holds an annual celebration for failed projects).

Someone once said, psychological safety is one of those things that you know when you have it and when you do not. I cannot agree more. It is easy to tell in meetings when one person dominates the discussion and there are few opportunities for people to speak up. Through body language, tone of voice or even how the atmosphere changes as soon as an individual enters the meeting, you can tell if people feel like they are walking on eggshells.

TIP #31

To develop a culture where everyone feels confident to speak up, prioritise psychological safety.

Psychological safety is fundamentally important to me as leader. Creating an environment where people disagree productively and can exchange ideas freely without judgement unleashes innovation, unlocks the benefits of diversity and allows companies to adapt swiftly and successfully to change.

Regard feedback as a gift

I am a big believer of the growth mindset. It forces us to acknowledge that we are all a work in progress and as a result, become more open to giving and receiving feedback. Research shows that although 95 percent of us think we are self-aware, only 10 to 15 percent of us actually are. This means the rest of us are either lying to ourselves, in denial or just not seeing ourselves clearly. This is why I see feedback as a gift.

While positive feedback keeps us motivated, it is constructive and honest feedback that helps us learn from mistakes and grow. I am extremely grateful to have worked with many good people, who have invested their time to provide me with constructive feedback. Sometimes this has been difficult to hear, but mostly it has been instrumental for my learning and growth. I am thankful for those who have invested in my growth in this way.

Personally, I have found that once colleagues/managers/clients know that I am keen to receive constructive feedback, they are generous with their time and "gifts". This can be a blessing and a curse. I recall messing up a global conference call held in the wee hours of the night (Australia time) with senior colleagues in New York. My manager (another fantastic mentor), who was also on the conference call, was quick to phone me – not once, but three times – to explain the ways I had messed up. Acutely aware of my mistakes, extraordinarily tired at 2am and in tears, I confessed on the third call that I could not take any more feedback at that moment. I can laugh about it now but you can be assured I have not ever messed up in the same way since.

Former Apple and Google executive Kim Scott calls it radical candour – providing feedback that is both direct and caring. It is about caring enough for someone to tell them what they need to hear today, so they can become better tomorrow. And it goes both ways. We need to have courage to ask for feedback and be open to it, knowing that it is because someone cares and wants the best for us.

TIP #32
Positive feedback keeps us motivated. But it is constructive and honest feedback (or radical candour) that helps us learn from mistakes and grow.

Scott gives a simple example of telling someone they have spinach in their teeth. Radical candour is pulling them aside and telling them quietly and kindly so they can fix the problem with minimal embarrassment. Likewise, if you have spinach in your teeth, you want to know. After all, you are the only person who can do something about it.

Nurture trust

One of the key learnings and proudest moments during the pandemic was seeing how my colleagues at Mercer came together to support not just one another but also our clients on challenges, from ensuring comprehensive healthcare measures for their employees to effective vaccination rollouts.

From connecting clients to healthcare partners, to supporting vaccination rollouts in their workplace in India, to helping clients arrange talks by doctors to educate their employees on the different brands of vaccines in Singapore, everyone rolled up their sleeves to support our clients in these critical, yet complex efforts.

For me, this speaks to the high level of trust our organisation has built with our clients. It is not something that just happens overnight, but has been created and nurtured over time by authentic, deliberate and observable behaviours.

In his book *The Speed of Trust,* Stephen Covey talks about two components of trust: character (integrity and intent) and competence (capability and results). Broken trust, he says, is always a failure of one or the other. Trust, he adds, has the power to create an organisation that is significantly more productive, nimble and effective. When trust is high, speed goes up because things happen faster and as a result, costs go down.

In my personal and professional experience, this has been true. As a young manager I tended to micro-manage (very annoying for everyone!). It took me some time to realise that when you have hired the best person for the job, you need to trust them to do it well – and they usually always will.

Similarly, at home, finding balance (and keeping family harmony) as parents requires trust. My husband might not do things the way I would like them to be done, but I trust that he does everything with love and great care (even if our children do look bedraggled at times!).

TIP #33
When trust is high, speed goes up because things happen faster and as a result, costs go down.

In times of uncertainty, trust matters — trust in ourselves, trust in one another and, for countless employees, trust in employers. In an interview, Eric Yuan, founder of Zoom, shared that it was trust that enabled his team to respond quickly to the pandemic and help millions of companies worldwide to go digital overnight. "Because every day is full of problems," he says, "and if trust exists, people get together more quickly to fix them."

Trust your team

O ne of the most disturbing phenomena that emerged in the shift to remote and hybrid work is how some companies have experimented with or taken to digital monitoring in their push for productivity.

We read of software technology that many companies used to track just about everything their employees did, from the number of keystrokes on their computers to computer activity by taking periodic screenshots. Technology aside, we also heard of managers who expected their employees to keep their webcams on at certain times to ensure they are not "slacking off".

This troubles me. Measuring productivity is not new and has its place. We use utilisation, for example, as a measure to inform us on how to run the business, know when we need to invest in more resources and prepare as best we can for an environment that is increasingly hard to predict.

While monitoring activity (or the lack of it) down to the second may increase productivity (for a short time), it will almost certainly stifle creativity, innovation and culture. Think about the employee who delivers more keystrokes an hour, but misses an opportunity to improve a workflow process simply because they have no time.

It will also almost surely erode the trust between employer and employee. There are few stronger signals that you do not trust someone than putting them under surveillance.

In working with leaders and teams across different industries and organisations throughout my career, I have seen how trust can, conversely, help people and companies grow beyond their expectations. I have witnessed how leaders and teams work through trust issues and get to the other side stronger and better. I have also seen how businesses can slow or stop without trust and that a culture without it usually permeates from the top of the organisation.

Organisations can do better than this. Productivity is important but trust needs to be the foundation for every relationship – between people managers and their team; between companies and their people.

TIP #34

While monitoring employee activity down to the second may increase productivity (for a short time), it will almost certainly stifle creativity, innovation and culture.

Form new connections and shared experiences

Typically, I prefer laid-back holidays where I have many pockets of quiet time to reflect, rethink and recharge. Studies show that taking time for silence restores the nervous system, helps sustain energy, and conditions our minds to be more adaptive and responsive – which is sorely needed given the complex environments in which we now live, work and lead. When I need to recharge in this way, I do like the mindfulness of a retreat where quiet reflection, healthy food and nature are very quickly restorative.

However, in the spirit of trying new things, one summer, I embarked on a jam-parked holiday where my family and I took the opportunity to reunite with friends we made around the world in Sweden and Italy. On that trip, I learnt to recharge in a different way and it resulted in different reflections.

At the reunion of my Hong Kong friends in Sweden and New York friends in Italy, we reconnected (mostly over great food) from daily Swedish 'Fika', to long, languid Italian dinners and gelato. A globally diverse group of friends who initially connected over new experiences living in new countries, we continued to share new experiences at our reunions – swimming in freezing Swedish lakes, exploring old Italian towns, and then biking and paddle-boarding through forests and canyons in Italy. It was high-energy, lots of fun and it reminded me of the importance of shared experiences and connections.

Being open to new connections broadens our perspective, helps us to keep learning and opens up new experiences and opportunities that might not have been possible. Shared experiences not only bring us closer but also build and nurture strong bonds for a lifetime – the same way they drive meaningful collaboration and super-charge high-performing teams.

TIP #35

Being open to new connections broadens our perspective, helps us to keep learning and opens up new experiences, opportunities and friendships that might not have been possible.

To be a senior business leader is a privilege and joy, but it can also be a lonely job sometimes. The personal connections that I have built with my colleagues and teams positively change this dynamic for me.

Spread contagious emotions

absolutely love leading and running businesses in growing markets. One of the many things I love about growth is that it creates new opportunities for colleagues and enables organisations to expand and welcome new colleagues onboard. New colleagues bring with them their own experiences, different perspectives and diverse points-of-view – all things that make us stronger and better as leaders and organisations.

I enjoy taking time to meet with new joiners. Listening to their stories and life experiences, I am invariably inspired by their diverse backgrounds and always learn something new. I love it especially when it involves learning more about cultures, customs and different behaviours.

Behaviour is learnt and it tells others a lot about us as individuals and as organisations. As behavioural scientist Vanessa Van Edwards shares, our behaviour – hand gestures, smiles, hellos – not only impacts how others perceive our confidence and ability but is also contagious[1].

If our emotions are contagious, how do we make sure that we are infecting people with the right ones? Van Edwards advises that

---

[1] Van Edwards, Vanessa. "You are contagious". YouTube, uploaded by Tedx Talks, 28 Jun 2017. https://www.youtube.com/watch?v=cef35Fk7YD8.

when you want to get people excited and engaged, use dopamine-worthy conversation starters. This includes using more hand gestures, offering authentic smiles and never picking up the phone in a bad mood. Instead of asking someone if they have been busy lately, which triggers their brain to think of all things negative – stress, a lack of me-time and so on – ask them if they are working on anything exciting recently. It creates pleasure for them and, according to science, makes you more memorable.

The idea of contagious emotions is interesting to me for many reasons, particularly the impact on culture in organisations. How we show up, listen, communicate and support one another can make or break someone's day. Put simply, we have the opportunity every day to positively "infect" one another with encouraging behaviours.

TIP #36
How we show up, listen, communicate and support one another can make or break someone's day.

PEOPLE

TO MAKE A DIFFERENCE, CELEBRATE DIFFERENCES ✉

Hello AMEA: The Domino Effect

 ⊗ **McGowan, Renee**
To:

Friday, 4 March 2022 at 10:00 AM

Hi everyone,

I hope your week went well. Many of us have been following closely the tragic events unfolding in Ukraine. This is a difficult time, especially for those personally affected, so let's continue to reach out and check in with one another. A dedicated Colleague Connect page has been set up so you can get the latest updates as well as ways to support colleagues affected and help, including a humanitarian relief fund. If you need support or know of someone who does, please reach out.

This week, I had the opportunity to visit Team Singapore (in their newly refurbished office!) and it was wonderful to spend some time with the team and our clients. Our strong women leaders based in Singapore, such as Peta Latimer, Godelieve van Dooren, Liana Attard and Joan Collar, were opportune reminders of the importance of celebrating International Women's Day next week. As I reflect on how far women have come – whether in education, the workplace or in politics – over the past decades, I'm reminded that it's the result of countless women and men who continue to speak up and be change-agents in the path to gender equality. As the world's youngest Nobel Laureate Malala Yousafzai once said, "If people were silent, nothing would change."

People who are willing to speak up for change are what writer and activist Luvvie Ajayi Jones calls **"the first domino"** in her TED Talk, "Get Comfortable with Being Uncomfortable". For a line of dominoes to fall, one has to fall first, which begins a chain reaction that travels down the line. For Jones, being the first domino is about embracing your discomfort and overcoming your self-doubt and fears – to be the one to take a leap that inspires others to follow. For many of us, the fear of change and failure is real. But not doing something because we're afraid to get started, keeps us from growing. As an organisation and as individuals, we all have the opportunity to be first-movers, to be the first domino. Big changes start with small acts of courage.

What's holding you back from being the first domino? I'd love to hear from you. And to all the strong, inspiring women in our midst, happy International Women's Day!

Take care.

Renée

Be a collaborative leader

A global survey of people from all walks of life conducted by the United Nations found, interestingly, that most people – regardless of their origin, gender or age – share common concerns and aspirations about the future. It also reported that most of us believe strongly in the power of working together to tackle the world's biggest challenges.

This brought to mind an insightful TED Talk on collaborative leadership by Lorna Davis, the former president of Danone, Kraft and Mondelez, where she shares how a prevalent hero culture in some organisations holds them back from solving real problems. The human desire to be a hero, she says, forces us to narrow our goals – to something neat and tidy (e.g. a profit and loss statement) – that we can take credit for. We choose the problems we want to solve – so we can look like heroes. But in reality, all the real and important issues that organisations and the world need to tackle require collaboration.

Heroes set goals that can be individually delivered and neatly measured, but collaborative leaders set goals that are important,

Be guided by the power of Ubuntu

but impossible for any one individual to accomplish on their own. Heroes reveal their goals when a path to achievement is clear but collaborative leaders invite others to co-create the plan. Heroes see everyone as a competitor or follower, but collaborative leaders understand they need others; they readily ask for help or often find ways to offer help.

TIP #37

Cooperation is more vital than ever, because when competitive instincts overtake cooperative mindsets, nobody wins.

My own experience is that collaborative leaders also have greater ambition – and they are more likely to be successful through collaborating with many to achieve that goal. There are many great leaders who have shown us this. John F Kennedy's bold ambition to put a human on the moon within a decade is an example that has always stuck with me. As he famously said, "We choose to go to the moon in this decade and the other things, not because they are easy, but because they are hard."

Be guided by the power of Ubuntu

Most business leaders know that their people are important. Companies across the globe are prioritising employee well-being, learning and development in light of the new skills, flexible working and digital transformation trends that are happening.

To me, it is a long overdue realisation that businesses cannot be all they can be, unless their employees are all they can be. And it reminds me of Ubuntu, a concept from South Africa that loosely translates to "I am because of you". In the words of Nelson Mandela, Ubuntu is "the profound sense that we are human only through the humanity of others; that if we are to accomplish anything in this world, it will in equal measure be due to the work and achievements of others."

For me, this has been a transformative way of working, living and leading. We can only be our best if our teammates are at their best. The better the people around us are, the better we become. When we encourage the greatness and success of others, we triumph together.

This powerful philosophy, which represents the power of connectedness and compassion, can change how we tackle some of the most pressing challenges of our time. It starts with gratitude and acknowledging the connections that we share. It is about being open and available to others and sharing selflessly what we have and know, because when we do better as a greater whole, we, as individuals, become better.

TIP #38

When we encourage the greatness and success of others, we triumph together.

Admittedly, this focus on the greater whole has been a tough learning point for me as a leader. I have been in the position where I was leading a strong team, but it was evident that one team member was not as strong or aligned with the team direction. I therefore spent a significant amount of time and effort on improving the team member's performance, but should have seen earlier that the fit could not be forced. In the end, I had to restructure the team but it was a hard realisation and decision for me to make.

Hire opportunity makers

n her TED Talk, Emmy-winning journalist turned motivational speaker Kare Anderson says we need more opportunity makers in our world – people who spot opportunities and actively connect the right people to seize them, better and faster than others.

Opportunity makers, she says, have three traits. They are constantly honing their strengths so when an opportunity arises, they can step up and be an asset to others. They constantly step outside their usual circles, so they can glean fresh ideas and leverage the strengths of others. Lastly, they are constantly on the lookout for opportunities where they can bring people and ideas together to make a greater impact with a better solution.

This really resonates with me. One thing I love about my job is that everyone is best at something. And when we bring all the people who are best at what they do together to solve a problem, imagine the impact that can have. Imagine what your business could accomplish if everyone were to become an opportunity maker to one another – to connect the dots, to bring the best talents together to find new solutions and solve difficult problems.

I once had an inspiring colleague, Natalie Truong, from whom I've learnt so much, say to me, "I love that we're smart at different things!" I laughed and agreed whole-heartedly; for me, this is the real power of diversity. In a poly-crisis world, where challenges companies face are increasingly complex and multi-dimensional, the need for diversity, particularly cognitive diversity, cannot be understated. A study highlighted by the *Harvard Business Review*[1] found that teams solve problems faster – and better – when they are more cognitively diverse.

TIP #39

By bringing diverse people who are best at what they do together to solve a problem, the impact can be significantly positive.

If this is what is needed to succeed in increasingly uncertain times, we need to encourage people to apply their different modes of thinking or make it safe to try things multiple ways. And this means creating a psychologically safe environment where everyone is safe to be themselves and to be an opportunity maker.

---

[1] Reynolds, Alison and David Lewis. "Teams Solve Problems Faster When They're More Cognitively Diverse." *Harvard Business Review*, 26 February 2021, https://hbr.org/2017/03/teams-solve-problems-faster-when-theyre-more-cognitively-diverse.

Know your bias

As we look at the global movements related to race, equality and inclusion, I am reminded of the impact of unconscious bias. It is dangerous as it can shape our views of someone, their ideas or even our behaviour, without us realising it. Are we drawn to people who look or think like us? When someone offers a perspective that does not fit our world view, are we uncomfortable? Have we treated anyone differently just because of their background?

When I first had the opportunity to recruit and build a small, new team for a new project, I selected great people who had held different roles with different educational qualifications. Sitting around a table, we all looked different – a diverse mix of gender and ethnicity. We worked well together, had fun and our team meetings were always efficient.

But over time, it became apparent that the team was harmonious, but not high-performing. We were doing a good job, but were not delivering the project and product to the highest standard. My realisation came during one team meeting – it was fun, efficient and there was quick unanimous agreement. Herewith was my problem. I had unconsciously recruited a team of individuals that was a lot like me. Sure, we were of different gender and ethnicity, but we were all about the same age and had similar socio-economic upbringings, schooling and early work experiences. Worst of all, we agreed with each other – a lot.

Today, with the benefit of this experience, I know that the best thing I can do as a leader is to create a workforce of truly diverse people, where difference is valued. For me, a great team is a varied mix of people, ages, ethnicity, cultures, backgrounds and beliefs. For me, a great team meeting is full of dialogue where everyone confidently voices and/or disagrees with a perspective. I love a respectful, loud and vocal team meeting, where debate is necessary and it is hard to make a decision. I know then that the decision we have made will be a better one.

TIP #40

Unconscious bias is dangerous as it can shape our views of someone, their ideas or even our behaviour, without us realising it.

Focus on inclusion and diversity

aving worked with leaders who have been great role models and believers of diversity and inclusion in the workplace and who have played a big part in my path to leadership, these are issues close to my heart. While the diversity dialogue has gained traction around the world in the past decade, inclusion is what I believe should be at the heart of the conversation.

In her TED talk, inclusion advocate Janet Stovall shares that "diversity is a numbers game. Inclusion is about impact. Companies can mandate diversity, but they have to cultivate inclusion". This truly resonates with me. Developing a diverse workplace is the (relatively) easy part and can be achieved with programs and targets. But to truly reap the benefits of diversity, we need to foster a culture where everyone feels safe and that their contributions are valued.

Inclusion does not just happen; we have to design for it. It starts with recognising that in a diverse workplace, differences exist and people require support in different ways. While equality calls for treating everyone the same, equity asks us to acknowledge that not everyone starts at the same place or has same needs. It is about giving each person what they need to succeed.

Take equality in a classroom, for example. It means every student gets the same resources and support – a calculator, a pencil and an assignment. It sounds good in theory but does not always work in practice. Equity means simplifying instructions or providing additional allowance for students who may not speak English as their native language.

Equity in the workplace can take many forms. It could be empowering employees with work education programs and ensuring equitable benefits like parental leave to fathers and mothers equally. It can also be enabling the inclusion of colleagues of different abilities, such as Mercer's AccessABILITIES program in India that provides meaningful careers for hearing-impaired colleagues supported through sign language interpreters and specialised technology.

TIP #41

Inclusion does not just happen; we have to design for it. It starts with recognising that in a diverse workplace, differences exist and people require support in different ways.

In many parts of the world, the conversation around diversity and inclusion still centres largely on gender; in large markets such as the US and the UK gender, racial and ethnic diversity all feature highly. However for companies to remain competitive and relevant, the conversation will quickly need to broaden and deepen to include ability, age diversity and increasing the representation of diverse talent in leadership positions.

Build a culture of confidence

The early 2020s marked by a global pandemic, geopolitical tension and social unrest have been an ultimate leadership test for CEOs and governments alike. We have all had to make hard choices, often times with insufficient data and in an environment of extreme uncertainty. In these circumstances, even the most seasoned leader will have some self-doubt as to whether the course of action was the best or right.

Likewise, I had my moments. In my first 18 months in Hong Kong in 2019-20, I was faced with more tough, time-sensitive decisions than I had ever experienced in my prior 18 years. Directing the business for the long term when you cannot see what is likely to happen next week is challenging. Making decisions that may impact the lives and safety of colleagues is agonising at times and self-doubt is inevitable.

In her TED talk, activist Brittany Packnett shares that confidence is the necessary spark before everything that follows; it is the difference between being inspired and actually getting started, between trying and doing until it is done. When we lack confidence, we are not in a position to do our best work, be our best selves and give our best ideas. And when that happens, nobody wins.

Building a culture of confidence starts with understanding that just like the diversity we embrace in our workplace, success comes in different ways, shapes and forms – and there should be many ways where people can demonstrate what they are good at.

As people managers, we also need to think about whether we are giving everyone on our team access to the same opportunities to stretch, shine and build their confidence. Often times, I have found that when you demonstrate belief in someone's ability to overcome a challenge or try something new, they start to believe in themselves. I have also had the unfortunate experience of being part of a team ruled by fear, and saw first-hand that when a manager displays doubt, both the confidence of the team and its individuals can be quickly eroded and performance suffers.

TIP #42

Confidence is the necessary spark before everything that follows; it is the difference between being inspired and actually getting started, between trying and doing until it is done.

Be the first domino

As I reflect on how far women have come – whether in education, the workplace or in politics – over the past decades, I am reminded that it is the result of countless women and men who continue to speak up and be change agents in the path to gender equality. As the world's youngest Nobel Laureate Malala Yousafzai once said, "If people were silent, nothing would change."

People who are willing to speak up for change are what writer and activist Luvvie Ajayi Jones calls "the first domino" in her TED Talk *Get Comfortable with Being Uncomfortable*. In her words, "silence serves no one". For a line of dominoes to fall, one has to fall first, which begins a chain reaction that travels down the line. For Jones, being the first domino is about embracing your discomfort and overcoming your self-doubt and fears – to be the one to take a leap that inspires others to follow.

She references this domino effect in relation to speaking up. It can be hard to do this, particularly if you believe your point of view is contrary to the majority. I have been in this situation many times and learnt a few hard lessons. In an early leadership position, where I was participating with an experienced group of senior leaders, I often felt that I did not have sufficient experience to speak up and weigh into a topic. I was more inclined to listen and observe, but became frustrated in situations where I thought no one was challenging the status quo.

My own feelings of being inexperienced relative to the leadership group around me, and my deference to colleagues with more years of experience, was impacting my ability to speak up. It also resulted in doubts about whether I should have the seat at the table I had been given. Thankfully, the CEO reminded me that I had earned and been awarded the seat because my work and perspective were valued. Over time with this group, I then learnt that by speaking up, there were others who also held a different view and started to share their perspectives more. Someone always has to be the first domino.

TIP #43

Being the first domino is about embracing your discomfort and overcoming your self-doubt and fears – to be the one to take the leap that inspires others to follow.

For many of us, the fear of change and failure is real. But not doing something because we are afraid to get started keeps us from growing. As an organisation and as individuals, we all have the opportunity to be the first domino. Big changes start with small acts of courage.

PATH

NO, YOU CAN'T BREAK UP WITH CHANGE ✉

Hello AMEA: Leading in Turbulent Times

⊙ McGowan, Renee

To:

Friday, 21 October 2022 at 10:00 AM

Hi everyone,

I hope you had a wonderful week. I've had a busy week trying to finalize our 2023 budget which got me excited about the dynamic parts of the world we live in. While global growth is slowing in aggregate - the IMF trimmed its global growth forecast to 2.7% - there are still some very bright spots in Asia and some parts of the Middle East.

The issues impacting global growth currently are uncertainty and volatility. However, it's in these highly uncertain, volatile environments that clients look to us to guide them through critical issues, including ensuring business resilience, managing risk, and attracting and retaining talent. It's also in these increasingly turbulent times that leadership is tested.

Our world is only going to become even more inter-connected, fast-paced and volatile, and this will demand new leadership skills and capabilities. Our future leaders will undoubtedly be different to the past, which is why we're deliberately investing – whether through the AMEA Leadership Program, Commercial Academy Masterclasses or leadership coaching – to nurture our leaders of tomorrow, so they can thrive in a world where uncertainty is the norm.

In a recent interview, author Jim Collins highlights five to-dos for leaders to find their way in turbulent times. Among the many good pieces of advice were to always prepare for the near-worst and to create a culture that asks "how do we learn from this?" instead of "who do we blame?" One thing that struck me was companies that did well in times of uncertainty had an unwavering focus on one key metric that moved their business – "a heartbeat march that kept them exerting a sense of self-control in a world that was out of control", as Collins puts it.

Ours is a growth march – a commitment to your growth and to developing leaders who will take our business to new frontiers because growth creates more opportunities for all. On that note, I'd encourage everyone to participate in the upcoming Marsh McLennan Learning Festival. And to everyone celebrating, happy Diwali!

Have a great weekend!

Renée

Embrace the discomfort of change

For some, change can be emotionally draining and uncomfortable, which is why we often resist it. But as performance expert and author Bill Eckstrom in his 2017 TEDx Talk said, "What makes you comfortable can ruin you, and what makes you uncomfortable is the only way to grow." He concluded this after having more than 50,000 coaching interactions in the workplace, leading him to conceive the idea of "Growth Rings". This is a concept centred on four different types of environments – chaos, complexity, order and stagnation – and understanding where you are closely relates to how well you will develop.

Although it never feels like it in the moment, discomfort challenges us to be better than we were before, to be stronger and to get out of our comfort zones. Having moved, lived and worked across eight cities – from Melbourne, Sydney, Yogyakarta, Singapore to London, New York, Hong Kong and now Dubai – in my life, I am no stranger to change. Sometimes I choose the change; sometimes the change chooses me.

I have always found change exciting, but it is not without its frustrations and discomfort. Earlier in my life, I was definitely a little hot-headed and reactionary in the face of change. But over time, I have learnt to take some quiet time to pause and think. Allowing myself to reflect instead of react helps me understand the different or new perspective, consider how I respond and challenge myself about what I can learn. I have found this gives me a sense of control and makes change a positive experience.

> **TIP #44**
> **Expect change to be uncomfortable, but use it as an opportunity to create new perspectives, acquire new skills and push boundaries.**

A key part of adapting to change is recognising how our attitude and behaviours ultimately shape our experience. I see change, big or small, as an opportunity to create new perspectives, acquire new skills and push boundaries. Often, taking the first step is the most difficult – but with equal measures of curiosity and courage, adventure awaits.

Ignore change at your own risk

Businesses that do well regularly review and change their business mix – in good times and bad. As the world embarks on a prolonged period of economic uncertainty, this rings true more than ever. There is a need to be as agile as the market; when clients demand change, the portfolio mix must be realigned to stay relevant.

But change takes courage – and conviction. History is littered with examples of companies that have failed to respond or simply ignored the winds of change and did nothing. Kodak, for example, did not pivot in time to lead the digital photography revolution, even though they were first in the world to develop a consumer digital camera. On the other hand, there are companies like Netflix, which made a big bet, shifting their core business model from DVD-by-mail service to embrace online video streaming and now, production of their own content.

Companies that successfully move their portfolio in the right direction rely on insights, not just intuition. Speed is also of the essence. But what is critical is focusing on creating value for their clients. When the world around us changes, success will not be found by doing the same things, the same way. Changes have to be made to the portfolio to focus on where they are most valued and needed by their clients.

I recall my excitement when asked to lead the Customer Experience for Mercer's individual investors. We already had a suite of outstanding services, but I was aware that external digital and customer experiences were taking great leaps in many industries and changing customer expectations. So, rather than simply doing the best that we knew within financial services, I joined a bootcamp at what was one of the leading experience businesses in the world, Zappos, led then by the late Tony Hsieh.

Zappos sells shoes and clothes online, but saw sales as the outworking of the customer experience they created and delivered, based on their customer insights. Despite being a vastly different business and market to ours, the practical learning that we took from the trip was highly relevant and valuable. Instead of just using customer data as insights to improve traditional customer experience and measures, such as wait-time and net promoter scores, we involved customers in designing the services they most needed, and built our culture around stories of their life. Our customers were not numbers to serve, we aimed to understand them – and how we had helped. The customer experience program we implemented after that trip was ultimately award-winning in our market.

TIP #45
In the face of change, be agile and bold and focus on creating value.

Being aware of the external trends and open to learning something adjacent to our core business turned out to be incredibly valuable. It required a growth mindset among the team, but also reflected positively on the then-CEO for the Pacific, Ben Walsh, who had the courage to support my participation in a bootcamp at Zappos – a business miles away from ours both in content and distance (its Nevada campus was over 13,000km from where I was based in Melbourne, Australia).

Get comfortable with "a state of flux"

The pace of change has never been as fast as it is today. There will only be more of that coming, not less. In her book *Flux: 8 Superpowers for Thriving in Constant Change*, futurist and World Economic Forum Young Global Leader April Rinne shares how to stay grounded even when the ground beneath is constantly shifting.

While most people easily embrace the change they choose (e.g. a new home or hair cut), they often struggle with what they cannot control or did not predict. To reshape the relationship with change, Rinne recommends embracing a "flux" mindset, which manages change by being grounded by personal values.

This requires slowing down to reflect on your values and consider what you may have missed. It allows the time and space to recharge, ensures decisions are unhurried and change can be embraced as opportunity, not threat. Thriving in change is also about knowing your "enough". As the world moves faster, driven by the mantra of "more", knowing that you are enough and how much is enough brings clarity about what truly matters.

I reflect on this flux mindset particularly when I need to make important decisions and often under significant time pressure. If the pressure is intense, it can be easy to make the first, or most obvious decision. Moving fast like this, without adequate reflection may see us trip up in haste and not see and understand everything adequately. This can result in either poor decisions, lack of clarity for the team or a team feeling disenfranchised and left behind.

TIP #46

Embrace fluctuation to make change your ally.

Thankfully, when making decisions under pressure, I have been surrounded by good bosses, mentors and team members who have reminded me to slow down to go faster. When I have done that, everything improves both for me and for my team, and with a clear decision made with conviction, we move faster.

Continue to self-disrupt

As the world navigated the ups and downs of the pandemic, it became clear that there was no returning to business as usual. The sudden disruption unleashed by the pandemic saw companies buckle under the strain, but it also spurred transformation and innovation – that might otherwise have taken years – in mere weeks and months.

Dyson designed a new ventilator in 10 days. Luxury giant LVMH went from perfume to hand sanitisers in just 72 hours. Gaming firm Razer set up a fully automated face mask production line in just 24 days.

At Mercer, we worked with insurers to implement telehealth appointments for employees of our clients and then broadened this to communities – a logistical feat achieved within days and well before COVID-19 even had a name.

While much of this change was forced upon companies by COVID-19, it has shown us all how quickly society can get creative, innovate and adapt in a time of crisis. It also got me thinking about how to keep up this pace and culture of innovation – even long after the pandemic. Now, more than ever, there is a need to step up and deliver practical solutions to the onslaught of challenges companies are faced with. How can the agility shown through the pandemic be harnessed? How can what is being delivered be reimagined to continue to remain relevant?

To thrive in the future, I am convinced that there is a need to continually self-disrupt as priorities shift faster than before. It requires diligent listening, finding ways to learn and understand pain points, priorities and where value can be added. It requires having a growth mindset – where the capability and capacity to learn and solve problems can be grown. And it requires the placing of all stakeholders at the heart of everything that is done – this demands ruthless prioritisation, focusing on activities of value and doing away with those that no longer serve our needs.

TIP #47

The world is constantly changing and we need to have a growth mindset and willingness to self-disrupt to adapt.

Co-exist harmoniously with technology

The pace of progress made towards producing a COVID-19 vaccine was astonishing. It is amazing what can be achieved when communities, experts, science and technology come together to solve the world's most pressing problems. What would normally have taken years (or decades), came to fruition in a matter of months. Upon reflection, it occurred to me how critical People + Technology are in the race for a vaccine, in addition to medical science.

People – experts of all disciplines – contributed to the way the treatment of COVID-19 was improved and the development of a vaccine. The world also saw truly innovative uses of technology to help it better manage the impact of COVID-19 across societies. For instance, MIT released results of an incredible study where Artificial Intelligence (AI) could detect asymptomatic COVID-19 infections via coughs recorded on a mobile phone.

I believe that technology does not drive change, people do. Unless steered by human ingenuity to create and act on new ideas, empowered by a culture that embraces innovation without fear, technology remains no more than a tool. It may even be capable of harm if it is not directed by human intelligence and guided by common human values. So how can people go about co-existing harmoniously with technology? An article I read in the *Harvard Business Review*, co-authored by Becky Frankiewicz and Tomas

Chamorro-Premuzic, provided a list of interesting suggestions[1]:

1. **Put people first** – Prioritise investing in talent who know how to leverage the technology and turn it into a useful tool.

2. **Focus on soft skills** – Hard skills like data analytics are important but in playing the long game, intellectual curiosity is one of the most important traits to look for in people.

3. **Drive change from the top** – Invest in top talent who can manage people and inspire them to work together as a team.

4. **Make sure you are acting on data insights** – Gather the data, put it to work and turn it into implementable decisions.

5. **If you cannot fail fast, make sure you succeed slowly** – Recognise that failure is a stepping stone to success and that investments in long-term strategies should ideally yield positive outcomes.

The challenge to co-exist harmoniously with technology will likely only get more pronounced as we see the world change dramatically with generative AI technology, digital currency and identities. Globally, few governments, institutions or organisations are doing enough to create the skills among people to be able to harness the technology. We must eliminate any prevailing fear and increase the willingness and speed at which institutions, people and society change, as change itself is inevitable and extraordinarily difficult to slow.

TIP #48
Technology does not drive change, people do.

---

[1] Frankiewicz, Becky and Tomas Chamorro-Premuzic. "Digital Transformation Is About Talent, Not Technology." *Harvard Business Review*, 6 May 2020, https://hbr.org/2020/05/digital-transformation-is-about-talent-not-technology.

Think again

Since the early 2000s, the accelerating pace of chance has forced the world to rethink everything it knows. But rather than wait for events in the world to expose blind spots in thinking and behaviour, organisational psychologist Adam Grant and author of *Think Again*, says the world can and should be more deliberate and proactive in rethinking and challenging its assumptions.

In his TED Talk *What frogs in hot water can teach us about thinking again*, he shared that while people are often happy to rethink their wardrobes or home decor, they tend to stick to their guns when it comes to goals, identities (a sense of who they are) and habits. With goals, they find reasons to convince themselves they are on the right path. With identities, they close their minds to potential alternative selves (e.g. I am only good at what I am doing now). And with habits, they find comfort in the ways they have always done things. Being good at thinking, he adds, often makes them worse at rethinking – the brighter they are, the harder it can be to see their own limitations.

In a rapidly changing world, the ability to rethink and stay open to change is more crucial than ever. And I think it takes an equal dose of courage and curiosity to rethink what we think we know. Rethinking does not mean having to always change minds. According to Grant, it just means taking time to reflect and staying open to reconsideration.

As leaders progress to more senior positions, this can get harder. I have observed some leaders who think they must have all the answers to have credibility with their team. Others have not had a genuine openness to really explore a different idea or will steadfastly cling to a sinking ship (or product idea) as they cannot concede defeat.

TIP #49

Be brave to rethink what you think you know.

Leaders must be deliberately self-aware to know "when to grit and when to quit" or when to walk away from old habits and embrace new ones. It is learning to say, "Perhaps, I do not have all the answers", to open the mind to new ideas (not just the ones that make you feel good); and to challenge thought process and conclusions.

Be rookie smart

Change can be exciting, but can also bring anxiety. Yet, as leadership expert Liz Wiseman points out in her book *Rookie Smarts: Why Learning Beats Knowing in the New Game of Work*, anxiety can be productive, driving us to learn as much as we can about new markets, their growth focus, challenges and more importantly, the people who will undoubtedly bring fresh perspectives, new ideas and an arsenal of expertise.

I remember how back in 2021, Mercer announced a restructure, which saw Asia, Middle East and Africa being combined into one portfolio that I would oversee. For me, it came with a pinch of anxiety around the responsibility to do my best for all the different stakeholders. However, it energised me to learn and focus on new ways to accelerate Mercer's growth. I knew that having all the regions represented at the Executive Leadership table (that I was going to be a part of) would bring global and local closer together to accelerate decision making and the pace of growth – a change I knew would help us respond with more agility to local needs and opportunities.

Of course, we do not stay rookies forever but Wiseman reminds us of the importance of having a rookie mindset, whether solving an old problem or taking on a new one. It forces us to not let what we know limit what can be imagined. Being a rookie, she says, means approaching tasks with fresh eyes, knowing that we do not have all the answers. It means being unencumbered by past ways of doing things with no limit to our thoughts or aspirations. And being on alert and in "seeking" mode the whole time, asking questions and gathering as much information as possible to make the best decisions.

TIP #50
Embrace a rookie mindset – don't let what you know limit what you can imagine.

By taking a step back and embracing a rookie mindset, I think new ideas for challenges or fresh possibilities for age-old problems can be found. With it, organisational breakthroughs can come from anywhere and anyone. And that is powerful.

Lead with productive paranoia

Jim Collins, in his book *Great by Choice*, wrote, perhaps fortuitously, "We believe there will be no 'new normal'. There will only be a continuous series of 'not normal' times." Then, Collins was studying why some companies thrived in the tumultuous 2000s and why others did not. I think the lessons are just as relevant today.

While companies and people do not thrive on chaos, uncertainty and instability, there are core behaviours of leaders that help them thrive in chaotic times. Successful companies, Collins and his co-author Morton Hansen found, were disciplined – in preparing for the next storm in the good and bad times, in leaning on empirical evidence for their big bets, and in their pursuit of long-term growth, no matter what. And it is the discipline to stay focused that helps them create the future – even when they cannot predict it.

Another behaviour Collins and Hansen identified is "productive paranoia", which I think is a great phrase. This is about keeping an eye on worst-case scenarios but without letting it overwhelm you. In fact, it should guide you to lead the way forward. Another idea is to allow evidence and research to affirm what your creative instincts are. Nothing should be done on a whim or because a colleague "felt" it was the right thing to do. Everything has to start with empiricism.

I was living in Hong Kong when the pandemic started in January 2020. Of course, it was not a pandemic then, but a virus largely contained to mainland China. While not alarmed at this stage, we had muscle memory from SARS, and had completed our first business scenario plans for Asia by mid-January. We created various ones for what the impact of the virus might be.

Based on these scenarios, which included external and internal analysis, we decided to move to a precautionary mode to protect our employees and business. We provided sanitary provisions for all colleagues (before wearing masks was even a thing) and clear guidelines for colleague health, safety and support. We reduced all discretionary expenses to protect against the possibility of significant loss of revenue and any resulting impact this might have on the business and our colleagues' employment. We figured the precaution – or productive paranoia – outweighed the risk and that if nothing transpired and the virus dissipated, we would have a slower start to 2020 in Asia than we had budgeted.

TIP #51
Planning and discipline are required to protect and thrive in chaotic times.

By March 2020, the world was in chaos but this disciplined decision-making process had helped us to protect the business and our employees. By April 2020, Marsh McLennan had implemented disciplined business continuity plans globally, and it was a proud moment when our Global CEO committed to all 85,000 colleagues that their jobs were secure in the thick of the pandemic.

Lean into discomfort and take action

Can you ever be ready to take on a challenge? Probably not, but in the face of one, it is important to be willing to have a go at it anyway. This is the mindset, Holly Ransom, author of *The Leading Edge*, says should be embraced, especially as the pace of change and the level of uncertainty, complexity and ambiguity continues to accelerate.

Readiness, she says, is a dangerous mirage. It is easy to convince yourself that you need something additional to be ready and fall into the trap of inaction, waiting for things to line up better, for the data to be more perfect or for the situation to be more stable. In fact, what should be done is to ask yourself, "How can we start with what we have right now and put something in motion?"

I can really relate to this. Professionally, I have at times found myself procrastinating on a decision – thinking that I need just one more data point to make an informed decision. In my personal life, I've often thought that "now is not the right time" or "I need to wait until next year when things will be easier". This thinking resulted in a few hard lessons – a business error resulted from my prolonged decision-making process (a.k.a. inaction); and another time, I missed an opportunity for a job I really wanted as I did not think it was the right time to put up my hand. I learnt that inaction did not help my career or my personal life and that running the race is how we learn and grow.

For some, taking action may mean picking up the phone to call a client. For others, it could mean registering for the class you have always wanted to. Whatever is holding you back, lean into the discomfort and take action.

TIP #52
Not ready?
Leap anyway.

Of course, taking action might mean you are starting before you feel ready (or before you are actually ready). However, very rarely have I seen this approach fail. There may be a bump or two along the way, but taking action and leaning into opportunity is a sure-fire way to grow.

Be RAD (Resilient, Aware and Dynamic)

The pandemic has caused what has been called the greatest workplace disruption in generations and its economic impact continues to linger with war, inflation, supply chain disruptions and market volatility. Despite this, there have been businesses that have grown and flourished.

This disruption will likely continue, but the world can and must adapt to it. In his book *Disruption Proof*, author Brant Cooper shares that companies that weathered the pandemic better than others were RAD – Resilient, Aware and Dynamic. They were able to read and act quickly on signals of change. They experimented rapidly and frequently – not just with their products and services but also with business models and processes. More importantly, they understood deeply their client needs and what drives them.

This was seen in how restaurants pivoted to home deliveries and cook-it-yourself kits. Automakers like Ford moved into the production of personal protective equipment for healthcare workers and first responders. Consumer goods giants like Unilever prioritised its packaged food, surface cleaning and personal hygiene products over skincare where demand had dipped.

Cooper helpfully shares five elements that contribute towards creating a RAD attitude, which he encourages to communicate to everyone across an organisation: empathy, exploration, evidence, equilibrium and ethics. He emphasises, "We don't want data to make decisions for us, but we certainly should use the output of our experiments and the insights that we glean from customers to help us create value."

TIP #53

Making great leaps forward takes courage and a willingness to try new things at a moment when others are just getting by.

Making great leaps forward takes courage and a willingness to try new things at a moment when others are just getting by. When shifting into high gear on a sustainable path of high growth, there is a need to be more RAD than ever. Be disciplined about focusing on the right growth opportunities that bring real value to stakeholders, prioritising investments prudently and purposefully.

Grow big, but act small

In her book, *Start Up Forever*, Sahar Hashemi highlights the importance of acting small (like a start-up) even when you are big. She contends that as companies grow, so does the fear of doing something that leads to "doing things the way we've always done them". From encouraging failure, to not waiting for "the big idea" but acting on small every day ideas, she shares practical tips for big companies to embrace an entrepreneurial mindset.

One tip I loved was to ensure you were always looking at your business through a customer or client's eyes. As businesses expand, they tend to get busier with internal management – HR, policies, financial reporting, compliance. In the business of management, it is important that we do not create bureaucracy that pushes out the client focus. A start-up mentality is about always keeping focused on knowing your client, understanding their needs, making it easier for them to do business with you – keeping clients at the heart of the business.

I like to think that at Marsh McLennan, I try to nurture a start-up mentality in a variety of ways, from the language we use, to the way we develop new solutions and advice. I am alert to language that screams tired or bureaucratic, for example, the classic phrase "we tried that before". A start-up mentality would not state this; it would likely explore what had been done before, why it had not worked and what could be different.

It is also a misstep to think that employees in large companies are not entrepreneurial. I have personally found that enabling employee ideas to be explored in small ways can create great things. I recall our teams coming together to do a 24/5 sprint to create a prototype – five days of non-stop work, rolling across four countries, to successfully stand up a prototype that was ready to be put in front of clients for testing on day six. This was just one inspiring example, developed and managed entirely by colleagues who had an innate entrepreneurial spirit that just needed to be nurtured and given space to flourish.

TIP #54

Running a big company? It is possible to nurture an entrepreneurial mindset and start-up culture.

Find your heartbeat march

The issues currently impacting global growth are uncertainty and volatility. However, it is in these highly uncertain, volatile environments that guidance is necessary to navigate through critical issues, including ensuring business resilience, managing risk and attracting and retaining talent. It is also in these increasingly turbulent times that leadership is tested.

The world is only going to become even more inter-connected, fast-paced and volatile, and this will demand new leadership skills and capabilities. Future leaders will undoubtedly be different from the past. This is why it is important for every organisation to invest in and nurture its leaders of tomorrow, so they can thrive in a world where uncertainty is the norm.

In a recent interview, author Jim Collins highlights five to-dos for leaders to find their way in turbulent times. Among the many good pieces of advice were to always prepare for the near-worst and to create a culture that asks "how do we learn from this?", instead of "who do we blame?"

One thing that struck me was companies that did well in times of uncertainty had an unwavering focus on one key metric that moved their business: a "heartbeat march that kept them exerting a sense of self-control in a world that was out of control", as Collins puts it.

While helming Mercer in Asia, I felt ours was a growth march. It was a commitment to the growth and development of leaders who would take the business to new frontiers because growth creates more opportunities for all. It was about providing valuable advice to our clients and with that, our people learnt more and had new experiences and opportunities, allowing them to grow too. As we were committed to our local communities through education, internship and community programs, our local communities grew too. This was our company's heartbeat and it was felt by everybody.

TIP #55
Develop your company's heartbeat march and ensure your leaders know its rhythm.

Map out bold futures

A lot of my time at work is dedicated to strategy – how to strengthen and shape the firm's future, invest in and develop people, differentiate ourselves from the competition and sustain high growth. All this gets set against the backdrop of uncertain and often volatile global trends and influences.

Spending time focusing on the future reinforces, for me, some of the views of leading foresight researcher Professor Jim Dator. He says that the world will only continue to change at a faster and more disruptive pace and predicting the future with certainty is impossible. In his article "Dator's Laws of the Future", he explains that we can only "forecast" alternative futures based on current trends in society, technology, politics and the economy. These alternative or preferred futures will continually change, so there is a need to keep adapting. More interestingly, he argues that any useful idea about the future should almost appear to be ridiculous in order to challenge existing norms.

To rise above disruption and uncertainty, I am convinced there is a need to define a bold future and act to make it happen. This applies to both growing a business and ourselves. Every action taken needs to work towards the person you want to become or business you want to build. And you need to constantly think and experiment in the space of the unimaginable to bring innovation to life.

I once declared that we had to double our business in three years, which seemed mathematically impossible, given prior growth rates. To the cynics, it was an unrealistic or even ridiculous future ambition. For me, the more ridiculous future was to assume we could only do what we had done in the past. Forecasting the future based on the performance of the past was a financially reasonable approach, but automatically limited our thinking of what was possible. Doubling our business would require us to think differently about the work we did today and what we should be building for tomorrow. It inspired us to aim to learn, grow and achieve more tomorrow than we had in the past – and we were capable of this. I never doubted it.

TIP #56

Do not limit your future to what you have achieved in the past. Be bold in your ambition and you will discover new ways to succeed.

PATH

YOU DON'T
KNOW IT ALL ✉

Hello AMEA: Are you an explorer?

 ⊗ **McGowan, Renee**

To:

Friday, 27 May 2022 at 10:00 AM

Hi everyone,

I hope you had a great week. I was so proud to read yesterday's <u>announcement of a planned merger between BT Super and Mercer Super Trust in the Pacific</u>. It's a great collaboration that will ensure better retirement outcomes for Australians and a wonderful example of how Mercer continues to grow.

This week, we also had the privilege of welcoming Martine in Dubai as she spent some time with business leaders on our strategy for the Middle East and also <u>a fireside chat where we got to know her better</u> from her worst subject in school (Biology!) and her favourite city in the world (Madrid) to what shifting into high gear means for the region (first, it's to believe we can do it!).

One great nugget of advice she gave to colleagues with C-suite aspirations is to always continue learning. It's among the <u>key building blocks</u> of our global <u>Journey to a Bright Future</u> and also core to our AMEA Growth Community, to <u>#goingplacestogether</u>. For me, the belief that I always have more to learn, that I can always improve has undoubtedly helped me grow both as leader and as a person. I don't always get it right, but when I do, staying curious and learning has given me the confidence to bring fresh ideas to the table, to challenge old ways of doing things and to keep pace with our fast-changing world.

John Hagel III, author of *The Journey Beyond Fear*, likens <u>lifelong learners to explorers</u>. Explorers, he says, are committed to making an impact in fields that excite them. They are excited when faced with unexpected challenges – and get bored when not challenged enough. They also seek out and connect with others who can help them get better answers faster. One thing that's also true of explorers is that they take charge of their own learning and development. As they move through their career, they take an ahead-of-time approach – rather than just-in-time – to learning.

I hope all of you are excited about <u>the launch of Degreed</u>; it's an intuitive learning platform personalized to the insights, expertise and skills you want to build, so you can use what you need when you need it. I encourage everyone <u>to log in and be an eager explorer today</u>. I look forward to hearing all your learning adventures. And if there's someone who has inspired your learning journey, consider nominating them for the <u>AMEA Growth Star award</u>.

Till next week, take care and have a wonderful weekend!

Renée

Inspiring Fireside Chat between Martin Ferland (CEO, Mercer)
and Tarek Lotfy (CEO, IMETA).

Embrace the growth mindset

When the going gets tough, it can be difficult to look for that silver lining – but this is precisely what leaders are expected to do. So how do you go about spotting and seizing the opportunities on the horizon, when you yourself are overwhelmed?

It all starts with our mindset. We live in a volatile and uncertain world, where we can easily feel every bad event is a crisis. This thinking goes nowhere fast, and a better approach is to embrace what Professor Carol Dweck calls a "growth mindset". This is a belief that talents and abilities can be developed through hard work and continual learning, including learning from failures. Her research shows that people with a growth mindset have a greater ability to thrive in even the most difficult situations because they view struggle and failure not as inability, but as an opportunity to emerge stronger, brighter.

In her book *Mindset: The New Psychology of Success*, Dweck writes, "Why hide deficiencies instead of overcoming them? Why look for friends or partners who will just shore up your self-esteem instead of ones who will also challenge you to grow? And why seek out the tried and true, instead of experiences that will stretch you? The passion for stretching yourself and sticking to it, even (or especially) when it's not going well, is the hallmark of the growth mindset. This is the mindset that allows people to thrive during some of the most challenging times in their lives."

I learnt the importance of a growth mindset the hard way. As a teenager, I put my hand up to complete a one-year high school exchange to Indonesia. I was excited, adventurous and very keen to explore and learn about a new culture and country. Arriving from suburban Melbourne to a bustling city in Indonesia, living with strangers and entering a local high school – all without knowing a word of the language – hit me hard.

I had been naïve and it was all harder than I expected and literally everything was different and foreign to me. If I or my parents had a fixed mindset, I would have upped and run back to Australia (as I did call back crying to come home on occasions). Instead, I was encouraged to push through, to embrace the differences and relish the experiences. I tried new food and activities, learnt the language and made new friends. Along the way, the growth mindset kicked in to think of what was possible. What has resulted is a lifelong love affair with Indonesia, its language, food, people and culture.

TIP #57

No matter how difficult the situation, a growth mindset will lead you to a better outcome.

Zoom in, zoom out

A s a CEO, most of my time at work is consumed with thinking strategically about and planning for the future. While charting a course for the future is critical, it is also important to keep an eye on the details: the "what, how and when" that needs to be planned and executed with discipline to make a strategy a success.

Having a winning strategy is only half the battle, especially in an environment where the big picture is constantly shifting. By grasping the details of what we do at work, client needs and the business we are in, we are positioned to execute flexibly and quickly, through ups and downs. This is where it is possible to deliver real value to clients and where businesses can thrive.

Harvard Business School professor Rosabeth Moss Kanter shares that effective leaders zoom in and zoom out. Both perspectives – worm's-eye and bird's-eye – she says, has its benefits and are needed for leaders to have a complete picture. Balancing the big picture with details ensures not just taking off, but taking off in the right direction.

This is not new. In the old days (back in 2001!), I was really fond of the concepts of adaptive leadership and leaders "standing on the balcony" – a management model conceived by Ronald Heifetz and Marty Linsky. They emphasised the need to "get off the dance floor" to prevent being overly mired in the details. "Leadership is an improvisational art. You may be guided by an overarching vision, clear values, and a strategic plan, but what you actually do from moment to moment cannot be scripted. You must respond as events unfold," they wrote, in an article for the *Harvard Business Review*[1].

TIP #58
Effective leaders constantly zoom in and zoom out to ensure they have the full picture and right direction.

I think "zoom in and zoom out" modernises this concept and is equally relevant today, as it was in 2001.

---

[1] Heifetz, Ronald and Marty Linsky. "A Survival Guide for Leaders." *Harvard Business Review*, 25 September 2020, https://hbr.org/2002/06/a-survival-guide-for-leaders.

Have fruitful friction

D o you have deathly quiet team meetings? Or are they often raucous? I prefer mine to be in between, where there is a healthy level of debate and discussion, as opposed to consensus all the time.

Ray Dalio, founder of Bridgewater Associates, writes about the importance of building a team that is comfortable with conflict and challenging each other in his leadership book, *Principles*. In his TED Talk, he shares why he shifted his decision-making attitude from "I'm right" to "How do I know I'm right?". He went on to surround himself with people who'd disagree with him to understand their perspective or have them stress-test his perspective. In short, the best leaders are focused on wanting to get it right, and not being right.

As a leader, I will be the first to admit that I do not always have the answers, especially given how our world is one of sustained uncertainty. What matters more is ensuring I am surrounded and supported by a great team who is willing to challenge one another's assumptions and beliefs, knowing that our end goal is finding the best outcome.

At Mercer, I had the privilege of being part of a diverse global executive team where discourse was common and encouraged. Mercer's Global CEO Martine Ferland – a leader and mentor I admire greatly – considers a good meeting as one where we have had "fruitful friction" – and where we come out of the meeting very tired. Respectful fruitful friction means we are using our knowledge, intellect and experiences to debate and challenge until we reach the right outcome. And when we leave the room (exhausted from the discourse), we leave aligned as an executive team on the right outcome.

TIP #59

As a leader, focus on wanting to get it right, and not being right.

It is only through transparency and promoting a culture where everyone feels empowered to provide constructive feedback and debate that we can truly stay ahead competitively and create better outcomes in each situation.

Are you really listening?

t is easy to underestimate the power of listening and overestimate our ability to do it. Listening as a skill is not new. In fact, it was brought to light as an important tool for change by psychologist Carl Rogers in an interesting article back in 1952. But listening skills, researchers say, have only declined over time. Amid smartphones, texts, tweets, chats, emails and other distractions, there is today a lot more talking, and, unfortunately, not enough listening. Research has shown that most people tune out during conversations about 30 percent of the time and retain at best 10 to 20 percent.

When listening, some are busy thinking about what to say next. Some listen only long enough to figure out if the other person's views are aligned with them. And then there are those who interrupt with solutions – often before a problem has been fully fleshed out. Personally, I have a problem with solutioning, as I have a natural tendency to start thinking of solutions when I am listening to people's problems – and I should just be listening!

There are simple steps that can be taken to become better listeners. Give 100 percent of your attention. Resist interrupting. Do not judge or impose solutions. And ask good questions, questions that benefit the other party and not your curiosity. While it may seem straightforward, listening is like a muscle that needs to be trained every day.

TIP #60
Remove all distraction, focus and truly listen – you will be amazed by what you hear.

When genuinely listening, you put yourself into the other's person shoes and tap into their frame of reference. Listen not just for what's being said but also for what's not being said – the underlying emotions and needs. Listening, says acclaimed negotiator William Ury in his TEDx Talk, has the power to transform the workplace, families and even the course of history.

When was the last time you took five minutes, put down your phone and truly listened?

Nurture a questioning culture

From 2013 to 2019 Mercer's Global CEO was Julio Portalatin. To my great fortune, we had a few opportunities to interact and over time, he became both my mentor and sponsor. Of the many things I've learnt from him, one of the most impactful is the importance of asking good questions. I had the privilege of observing the way he as a leader would engage with teams around the world, asking interesting questions that extracted great insights. He would also challenge me to think differently via the questions he would ask.

I remember after one important meeting and presentation to a senior executive team, I was despondent and disappointed with the outcome. I was having a moment (okay, it was actually a rant) about the decision made in a meeting. I did not agree with the decision, had expressed my views but the decision was not aligned with what I thought was the optimal outcome. I had been hoping for a bit of sympathy or even agreement from my mentor ("yes, of course, that's not the best decision etc."). Instead, he was quiet and simply asked one question, "Why do you think that was the outcome agreed?"

The question forced me to think about the issue, stakeholders and meeting in a different way. To be able to answer the question, I had to unpack who was involved, their experiences, perspectives and then all the dynamics of the pre-work and the meeting. It was a powerful moment of reflection on both the decision (the *why*), the perspectives and my role in the decision-making.

I have learnt that asking the right questions helps to organise our thoughts around what we do not know and allows us to view the same situation from different angles. This is advice given by journalist and author Warren Berger, who wrote the book *A More Beautiful Question* in 2014.

In it, he emphasises the importance of asking questions in the right sequence too – asking "why, what if and how", in that order, can help one advance through three critical stages of problem-solving. "Why" questions are ideal for coming to grips with an existing challenge or problem – helping us understand why the problem exists, why it has not been solved already, and why it might be worth tackling. "What if" questions can be used to explore fresh ideas for possible improvements or solutions to the problem, from a hypothetical standpoint. When it is time to act on those ideas, the most effective types of questions are practical, action-oriented ones that focus on "How": how to give form to ideas, how to test and refine them with the goal of transforming possibility into reality.

TIP #61
Asking the right questions allows us to view the same situation from different angles and reorganise our thoughts.

His research also found that a questioning culture fuels curiosity and creativity, breeds empathy and understanding and often draws out ideas and solutions that may have been taken for granted or missed. These are pertinent points, especially useful since we cannot afford to be complacent given the world we live in; we must keep learning what is new and anticipating what is next – and a good question might just help do that.

Exercise your contradiction muscle

Throughout my career, I routinely have to make difficult decisions, even as I try to balance being committed to and confident of an organisation's continued business growth and the professional development of the people I lead. More often than not, there are external headwinds and the operating environment is challenging, where only so much can be predicted and prepared for in advance.

An article I read on cognitive dissonance truly resonated with me just as I was wrestling with a series of strategy decisions[1]. This is the mental conflict you feel when your beliefs are contradicted by new information. The decisions were around where to continue investing, where to start new investments and where to accelerate investment.

I had a strong conviction about the investments that were being made. I believed they were the right ones for the business to grow sustainably for the long term. On the other hand, I could not ignore the fact that the business environment in some areas had changed, which meant higher risk and often a potentially longer road to ROI. This translated into me having to do an ongoing evaluation of the short-term growth needs, while building for the long-term, including

---

[1] Ragbir, Lise. "What if We Believed Anything Was Possible?" *Yes Magazine*, 4 October 2022, https://www.yesmagazine.org/opinion/2022/10/04/psychology-truth-cognitive-dissonance.

how that time frame was defined. It required tough decisions to be made – to pause, continue or double down.

The article was a timely reminder of the need to stay open to new ideas and information, even disconcerting ones, by "exercising our contradiction muscle". The author, Lise Ragbir, writes, "Since we all experience cognitive dissonance, the phenomenon provides us with a collective opportunity to exercise this contradiction muscle in small, low-stake ways. Such a thought exercise can be a means of strengthening our ability to resolve inner and outer conflicts in preparation for bigger challenges."

TIP #62
Keep cognitive dissonance at bay by exercising your contradiction muscle.

Had I lost my ability to adapt, to move with the environment, to embrace new beliefs and reshape old ones, I would have lost my capacity to grow. It was a moment I gave myself a pat on my back (yes, it's okay to do this) for choosing the harder path that ultimately led to personal and professional growth.

Learn, unlearn, relearn

Lifelong learning is a term heard frequently. So being asked to unlearn feels somewhat counterintuitive. Still, this action is more pervasive than we realise. A good example is how during the pandemic, we had to exit our comfort bubbles by using more technology and working remotely instead of in an office. Many of us were forced to adapt to new technologies, which helped us to collaborate better, albeit with some practice and patience.

As a *Harvard Business Review* article puts it, "Unlearning is not about forgetting. It's about the ability to choose an alternative mental model or paradigm."[1] Unlearning is first about recognising that what got us here will not get us there. It requires that we continually challenge our own best thinking and assumptions (e.g. does my leadership style still work in the remote setting?), be constantly curious about our blind spots (e.g. how do we know this is the best approach?) and stay humble enough to listen to other perspectives.

I recall once acquiring a small company and as we integrated, I met the new team and engaged with them openly, transparently and collaboratively. I peppered them with questions and then proposed how we would work together, what the next steps might be and how we would approach those next steps together and

---

[1] Bonchek, Mark. "Why the Problem with Learning Is Unlearning." *Harvard Business Review*, 3 November 2016, https://hbr.org/2016/11/why-the-problem-with-learning-is-unlearning.

collaboratively. There was a lot of nodding of heads, polite feedback and answers to my questions.

At the end of the meeting, I queried if there was anything else and one of the team members bravely said, "Thank you for meeting with us, but I'm not clear about what exactly you want us to do?" In short, I had taken the style and approach that worked in my organisation and automatically assumed it would be the same for the acquired company. I had not stopped to listen, learn and understand the differences in our cultures and to think about how we would come together effectively, in a way that could bring all teams members in. It was a very impactful learning moment.

TIP #63

To grow, be open to learn, unlearn, and relearn. Continually challenge your own best thinking and assumptions, be constantly curious about blind spots and stay humble to listen to other perspectives.

Futurist Alvin Toffler once wrote, "The illiterate of the 21st century will not be those who cannot read and write, but those who cannot learn, unlearn, and relearn." Every day, we have a choice to go through life or grow through life. Like me, I hope you choose growth.

Reimagine learning

Dutch business theorist Arie de Geus famously said in the 1980s, "The ability to learn faster than your competitors may be the only sustainable competitive advantage." While his advice is more than 30 years old, it could not be more relevant today. With the ever-increasing pace of change today – and the unpredictable nature of its impact (think generative AI), how well we respond to the constant shifts in how we live and get work done boils down to our ability and desire to learn.

It all starts with reimagining the idea of learning. Beyond corporate learning portals and on-demand learning platforms, which often get side-lined by the urgency of work, we need to embrace learning in the flow of our everyday work. This could be as simple as paying attention to the tactics and techniques your colleague uses while negotiating with a client, getting feedback on your presentation skills, bookmarking articles on your "to-learn" list or starting your day with 30 minutes of learning as you do with exercise.

While working on this book, I learnt all about publishing and what it takes to evolve a kernel of an idea, all the way to a 200-page tome. I am also appreciating how much work is involved and have incredible admiration for all the wonderful authors in the world. I realised I enjoyed it so much I am even thinking of starting a new book project soon.

I am definitely an experiential learner. Doing a formal course of study does less for me than learning from new experiences and challenges, being able to observe and meeting new and interesting people.

TIP #64

Opportunities to learn are everywhere – you just need to open your mind to them.

It may come easier for some, but I think if we were all a little more curious and paid a little more attention, we would find that opportunities to learn are everywhere. Just as the way we work has changed, so must our ways of learning. I encourage everyone to start today, even in a small way.

Reach for resilience when relearning

Have you heard of Christine Ha? She is the first-ever blind contestant and winner of MasterChef America Season 3 in 2012. Her story is an inspiring one. She triumphed over 30,000 home cooks to clinch the title, walking away with a US$250,000 cash prize and a cookbook deal. I hosted a fireside chat with Christine at an internal Mercer event in 2022.

Gordon Ramsay, a MasterChef judge and celebrity chef himself, said, "The lady has an extraordinary palate, a palate of incredible finesse. She picks up hot ingredients, touches them, and she thinks about this image on the plate. She has the most disciplined execution on a plate that we've ever seen. But the palate is where it's just extraordinary. And honestly, I know chefs with Michelin stars that don't have palates like hers."

That Christine could defy the odds to not only conquer MasterChef but also author a cookbook (which became a *New York Times* bestseller) and open two restaurants were already incredible feats to be proud of. But what struck me the most was how she had to refine and relearn cooking all over again as her eyesight gradually faded with the years. In spite of that, her spirit remained indomitable. "Losing my vision taught me to be more fearless in life. If you can't see how steep the mountain is, then you can't fear it," she said.

What Christine went through was uncomfortable, difficult and as *Harvard Business Review* co-authors Helen Tupper and Sarah Ellis, say, it takes resilience[1]. Relearning, they add, is "recognising that how we apply our strengths is always changing and that our potential is always a work in progress". The ability to constantly adapt and relearn will be critical in the face of changing tides.

TIP #65
If Christine Ha can lose her eyesight and still win MasterChef America, we should all feel confident to relearn anything.

---

[1] Tupper, Helen and Sarah Ellis. "Make Learning a Part of Your Daily Routine." *Harvard Business Review*, 4 November 2021, https://hbr.org/2021/11/make-learning-a-part-of-your-daily-routine.

Admit you don't know

A few years ago, I took a digital quiz where my team members and I were pitted against each other. Unfortunately, I came last – I did not respond quickly enough (response time was limited) or accurately enough, and I just barely passed with five out of 10 questions right. All my team mates did better than me – a hard pill to swallow for a competitive person, but a wonderful reminder of the importance of surrounding yourself (in work and life) with diverse people who know things you don't and to never stop learning.

Nobel Prize-winning economist Daniel Kahneman, who spent more than 60 years researching human behaviour, concluded that people are always much more confident of what they think they know than they should be. As he writes in his book, *Thinking, Fast and Slow*, we have an "unlimited ability to ignore our ignorance". The illusion of knowledge is often more dangerous than ignorance.

As leaders, pressure is a constant companion, including to always have all the answers. But I think there is a huge upside to admitting "I don't know". Not knowing is saying yes to going outside of your comfort zone, to embracing new skills and knowledge, and to leaning on and learning from your team.

TIP #66
Ignore your ignorance at your own risk.

As with all things new that are being picked up and learnt, it is inevitable to feel clumsy, make mistakes and ask what may seem at times silly questions. And that is okay. You will be bad at this for a while until you get good at it. If you ever feel discouraged, remember that I came in last on that first digital quiz, but did move up the ranking over time!

Be an explorer

The belief that I always have more to learn, that I can always improve, has undoubtedly helped me grow both as leader and as a person. I do not always get it right, but when I do, staying curious and learning has given me the confidence to bring fresh ideas to the table, to challenge old ways of doing things and to keep pace with our fast-changing world.

John Hagel III, author of *The Journey Beyond Fear*, likens lifelong learners to explorers. Explorers, he says, are committed to making an impact in fields that excite them. They are excited when faced with unexpected challenges – and get bored when not challenged enough. They also seek out and connect with others who can help them get better answers faster.

One thing that is also true of explorers is that they take charge of their own learning and development. As they move through their career, they take an ahead-of-time approach – rather than just-in-time – to learning. They are drawn to environments that will complement their ambitions, including connecting with the people who can motivate, celebrate and cheer them on. For as much as these sound like minor adjustments, they could lead to grand endings. "Smart moves, smartly made, can set the big things in motion," said Hagel.

I try to always be an explorer and am deliberate about how I do this. I listen to podcasts, read books and articles from diverse sources. But I also make tactical plans for learning in the way I like, such as attending one external event each month, where I am exposed to the views of subject matter experts. I arrange meetings with two new people – colleagues, clients or new acquaintances – each week to learn their story, their experiences and perspectives. Doing something non-work related also helps to cement what I have learnt during the day. For instance, on business trips, I love to take one evening to visit an art gallery or museum; I tend to come away refreshed and full of ideas. Lifelong learning, I realise, comes in many forms.

TIP #67

An explorer never stops learning.

PROGRESS

TAPPING YOUR CREATIVE GENIUS ✉

The Asia CEO Update: Designing our Future

McGowan, Renee
To:

Friday, 11 September 2020 at 9:00 AM

Hi everyone,

I hope you had a fulfilling week. Today marks an important day in Marsh & McLennan's history as we remember and honour the 358 colleagues we lost in 2001. Through our Global Days of Service program, we honor these colleagues by making a meaningful difference for our communities around the world – join me in participating in some of these events this month.

This week, I had the privilege of attending and facilitating sessions at Marsh & McLennan's Better by Design event. While the 72-hour event has now concluded, the sessions and on-demand videos are available to all colleagues and I encourage you to take a look. I was inspired by some of the world's great thinking on how we can use our experience this year to truly design a better future. Our own Martine Ferland hosted a discussion with Her Majesty Queen Rania Al Abdullah of Jordan and some of her thoughts really resonated with me. Specifically, she concluded the discussion reinforcing that we often hold ourselves back: 'I am good at x; I'm not great at y' and so on. We are confined only by the walls we build in our minds and we have the ability to learn and change.

The event encouraged me to think about design, creation and innovation. While we are no stranger to the "Steve Jobs", "Jack Ma"s and "Sheryl Sandberg"s of the world, it's a myth that entrepreneurs are the key drivers of innovation in society. The fact is, says innovation expert and author of Driving Innovation from Within Kaihan Krippendorff, over 70% of transformative innovations are conceived by intrapreneurs (employees in companies) and without it, we'd not have mobile phones, personal computers or email today.

This is due in part, he explains, to the advantages intrapreneurs have: scale that entrepreneurs can't easily match; access to multiple capabilities under one roof; resources their company has to invest and the ability to diversify risks. This excites me because what it means is that each one of us has the opportunity to change the world without quitting our jobs.

Unlocking the spirit and power of intrapreneurship takes work. It demands adopting an act-learn-build rather than a prove-plan-execute approach, an environment where disruptive business ideas are born in hallways, not boardrooms and nurturing agile teams, not silos. Winning ideas, he says, meet at the crossroads of market need, company need and passion. Passion for seeking out problems and finding solutions; passion for our job and responsibilities, showing care and persistence as though it were our own business; and passion to see each barrier not as a reason to give up but a problem to solve. Did you know Steve Wozniak was rejected FIVE times at Hewlett-Packard for his idea, which later became Apple?

As we look to reinvent ourselves, what can I and the Asia leadership team do to encourage intrapreneurs at Mercer? How can we provide the right resources or foster the right environment so you can design our future? Share with me and the leadership team over a virtual cup of coffee or send us an email. I'm excited to hear from you.

Have a lovely weekend – and if you haven't downloaded the Brighter Together app, check it out. There are some great recipes, ideas for exercises and useful information like our Employee Assistance Program all in local languages.

Renee

Her Majesty Queen Rania Al Abdullah of Jordan shared insights on the impact of the pandemic on women.

Better by Design

Anticipate (and solve) problems before they occur

I have had the privilege of attending and hosting sessions at the World Economic Forum's Davos conference in the past. It is always incredible to see and experience the phenomenally bright minds of individuals, organisations and institutions coming together to find answers to the world's most pressing problems – geopolitical tensions, war, climate and sustainability, economic volatility and food security, just to name a few. Interrogating the issues can sometimes be overwhelming, but I see an opportunity for us to think upstream, to look at ways to prevent problems rather than simply react to or solve them.

In his book, *Upstream: The Quest to Solve Problems Before They Happen*, Dan Heath shares that when we shift our energies upstream, we stop dealing with symptoms of problems but fix them instead. This, he says, applies to societal problems (chronic diseases, homelessness, famine) as much as business ones (client turnover, employee disengagement, gender disparity).

The idea may seem a simple one, but, he argues, as humans, we have "a strong urge to put off work on tomorrow's problems in favour of today's, even when tomorrow's problems may be far more serious". Solving today's problem (catching the criminal) sees immediate, tangible results, but upstream work (crime prevention) is far more difficult to measure. For us to get out of this cycle of response, we first need to overcome barriers of problem blindness ("I don't see the problem"), a lack of ownership ("this problem isn't mine to fix") and tunnelling ("I can't deal with the problem right now").

I have had to work on "upstream" a lot in recent years. When COVID-19 hit China in January 2020, I was leading Mercer's business in Asia and China was part of my portfolio. We had to consider how significant the virus was likely to be for the team and business based there, and what, if any, action should be taken. While "wait and see" would have been easier at the time, given all the other business priorities, we instead tried to go deliberately upstream.

TIP #68

Think upstream: look at ways to prevent problems rather than simply react to them.

We learnt as much as we could about the virus (it did not have a name at that time); we built scenario plans for the possible impact on colleagues and the business if this impacted China and moved to other countries. Most of the scenarios were full of uncertainty, each more alarming than the other, which prompted us to make business changes immediately. Of course, we never could have imagined how the world – and our lives – would be thrown into turmoil by the virus, but those tough early decisions and planning really helped the business weather the pandemic well.

As one *Wall Street Journal* columnist puts it, "One lesson from the coronavirus is that we need leaders who prevent crises more than we need managers who scramble to handle them."[1]

---

[1] Walker, Sam. "Covid-19 was a Leadership Test. It Came Back Negative." *The Wall Street Journal*, 14 March 2020, https://www.wsj.com/articles/great-leaders-are-killjoys-nags-or-neuroticsuntil-theres-a-pandemic-11584144175.

Reframe perceived obstacles

In his book *The Art of Possibility* and the corresponding podcast interview, Benjamin Zander, founder and conductor of the Boston Philharmonic Orchestra, talks of the power of focusing on possibilities surrounding us in any situation. Slipping into the default mode of focusing on limitations – many of which he says are assumptions we make (whether it is the fear of failure, the feeling we will not make a difference or comparing ourselves with others) – we restrict what we can accomplish.

Admittedly, it takes discipline to constantly and consciously reframe what we perceive as obstacles and choose possibility. Standing in the world of possibilities allows us to see and bring out the best in everyone. My daughter was once required to write an essay about advice she had received from a role model in her life. She wrote about a time when she was starting a new school in a new country and was understandably overwhelmed with nerves and apprehension. In her mind, she had played out every worst-case scenario of the school environment and her schoolmates.

According to her, when she came to me with her concerns, I asked her to think about and visualise the very best case scenario, and then focus all her attention and thoughts on that. I do not recall when exactly it was, but I had a proud-mum moment reading the essay and was reminded how it important it is to reframe perceived obstacles.

Zander highlights that the conductor of an orchestra is the only musician that does not make a sound but they have a lot of power; and the power comes entirely from their ability to get their players to provide the best sounds they are capable of – an important lesson in leadership we can all learn. "I realized that my job is to awaken possibility in others," said Zander.

TIP #69

Don't focus on the limitations of a situation, hone in on the possibilities instead.

Circumstances are not what hold us back; our mindset does. It is important to embrace possibilities – to see failures as stepping stones to success and obstacles as opportunities for growth.

Solve problems creatively the *jugaad* way

n 2022, I was privileged to be a judge at the 13th Youth Entrepreneurship Competition organised by INJAZ UAE, a member of Junior Achievement Worldwide. In going over their proposals, listening to their pitches and speaking to the high school students, I was not only impressed by their ideas but also their focus on businesses that can make a positive impact in the world. These young people were proposing business and technology solutions to solve for issues such as improving energy consumption in homes, right through to enabling communication between sign language users and non-sign language users. It was inspiring!

Being a witness to all that innovation reminded me of *jugaad*, a Hindi word which loosely translates to creative problem-solving or improvisation by using available resources. Travel to India and evidence of it is pervasive: coat hangers twisted into all sorts of shapes to make TV aerials, or running a car to power a home when there's an electricity outage. In fact, so compelling is the concept that it has made its way into the corporate parlance.

In their book *Jugaad Innovation*, the authors Navi Radjou, Jaideep Prabhu and Simone Ahuja argue that companies often over-engineer products through time-consuming processes, when they should keep things simple and concentrate on solving real problems instead of creating demand. The *jugaad* approach is bottom-up, agile and, most importantly, centred on delivering greater value for clients.

Reading this book was an "aha" moment for me, a realisation that I have been guilty of over-engineering unnecessarily. While a proponent of innovation, I was often reticent to invest in an idea until we had the ideal environment – it had to be the right time (no conflicting priorities), we had to have

TIP #70
Learn the art of *jugaad*: creative problem-solving or improvisation by using available resources.

sufficient capital investment and more importantly we had to have the capacity to devote to development. In doing this, I was actually over-engineering the decision-making process and making it unrealistic. Instead, I should have ensured we operated with greater agility, starting small by focusing on the client or the problem, and using available investment and capacity to execute. You can be sure that I've kept the *jugaad* way front and centre since.

Become antifragile

n his book *Antifragile*, scholar Nassim Taleb, who also coined the "Black Swan" metaphor, lays out the difference between being robust and being antifragile. "Antifragility", he says, "is beyond resilience or robustness. The resilient resists shocks and stays the same; the antifragile gets better." The key to thriving is not in avoiding disruption or chaos, but embracing the idea that stress – whether in the form of volatility or uncertainty – makes us stronger. Organisations and individuals that build themselves not just to withstand crisis, but to thrive and grow with adverse situations, are the ones that will last longer and grow faster.

Nature and the history of business provide many examples of the antifragile. Without stress, our muscles, abilities and willpower will atrophy. When we expose our immune system to a small quantity of a disease, it adapts, learns how to fight it, and becomes stronger. From the business world comes examples like how Netflix overcame digital disruption, going from a floundering DVD mail subscription service to the world's largest subscription streaming service today.

In my own career and personal life, I've realised that I have grown the most when I have been thrown out of my comfort zone and confronted with fresh challenges. As a young exchange student in Indonesia, I was completely out of my comfort zone (I could not even speak the language initially) and wanted to go home to my mum! Similarly, every new role I have taken has challenged me professionally – there is almost always a three-month (minimum!) period where I am lost, overwhelmed and wondering how I can make this work. But these moments, while hard, have been my greatest opportunities to grow and learn.

Becoming antifragile is not always easy. It demands that we stop thinking that our tomorrows are likely to be very much like our yesterdays. It forces us to rethink our old habits and ways of working, to experiment and not fear failure. And it requires us to continuously cultivate strength, to keep learning and solving problems, even when we are in a strong and good position, because no one knows when the next crisis might hit.

TIP #71

The key to thriving is not in avoiding disruption or chaos, but embracing the idea that stress – whether in the form of volatility or uncertainty – makes us stronger.

In a world where unpredictability and chaos are the norm, becoming antifragile is more important than ever. Antifragility is fuelled by unity. On our own, people or businesses may be fragile, but when we come together, we gain strength and become unbeatable, making a bigger impact.

Unleash your inner rebel

Have you heard of rebel talent? It is coined by Harvard Business School Professor Francesca Gino and describes people who constantly challenge the status quo and explore new ideas for positive change at work. In her bestseller *Rebel Talent: Why it Pays to Break the Rules at Work and In Life*, Gino argues we need to unleash the rebel in each of us. Sticking to what is safe and familiar, and keeping things the way they have always been is comfortable, but it also means nothing ever changes. When no one raises their hand or asks difficult questions, progress often comes to a standstill.

Being a rebel at work, Gino explains, is not about breaking the rules just for the sake of breaking them but to innovate and invent better ways of doing things. When we unleash our inner rebel, we are more engaged and fulfilled at work. Companies that embrace rebel talent inevitably achieve better outcomes. Not sure how to recognise such individuals? They all embody the traits of novelty, curiosity, perspective, diversity and authenticity.

"Rebels are well aware of how stereotypes may influence their actions. They actively fight against them and against conventional social roles. Rebels put themselves among people who think differently or who might have a different perspective. This allows them to leverage their differences and, in a sense, train their minds to avoid holding stereotypical views in the future," said Gino, in an interview with *The Harvard Gazette*[1].

TIP #72
Embrace rebel talent to innovate and invent better ways of doing things.

All of us have the opportunity to tap into our inner rebel to make a difference, to spur innovation and to inspire those around us. It is certainly something I aspire to. Even if the outcome may not be what I wanted or expected, I know at least I have tried.

---

[1] Pazzanese, Christina. "Unleash your inner rebel." *The Harvard Gazette*, 21 October 2021, https://news.harvard.edu/gazette/story/2018/05/in-an-age-of-constant-change-it-pays-to-be-a-rebel-harvard-author-says/.

Make the impossible possible

n 2021, I was incredibly inspired by an article in the *Harvard Business Review* where Pfizer CEO Albert Bourla recounted how he challenged his colleagues to "make the impossible possible"[1] – to produce a COVID-19 vaccine in record time. Getting thousands of employees to believe they could do it, he said, was the most challenging. Their journey to producing 300 million doses of their vaccine in just over a year is fascinating as it is motivating. In it, I believe, are lessons we could all use in our lives and work.

1. **Don't be afraid to think big** – In an interview with the *Wall Street Journal*, Bourla said, "I always try to shoot for the stars, because I know that even if you miss it, you will land somewhere on the moon". I could not agree more.

2. **Always think outside the box** – We cannot expect different results if we keep doing the same thing. When presented with solutions, Bourla pushed his team to provide options that have not been done before. After a few months, he says, it became a habit.

---

[1] Bourla, Albert. "The CEO of Pfizer on Developing a Vaccine in Record Time." *Harvard Business Review*, Magazine (May–June 2021), https://hbr.org/2021/05/the-ceo-of-pfizer-on-developing-a-vaccine-in-record-time.

3. **Purpose pushes us to achieve the extraordinary** – Few of us know what we are capable of until we are confronted with the greatest challenges of our lives. Pfizer's mission to "breed breakthroughs that could change patients' lives" was what galvanised employees to work harder than they had ever before to achieve the impossible.

I think these lessons apply to organisations and each of us as individuals. These are some of the core elements of a growth mindset. I do not think I would be the person I am today if my parents had not continually reinforced that my boundaries for learning were limitless. I did not appreciate it at the time, but now I am trying to do the same thing with my own children!

TIP #73
Once you understand that the boundaries for learning are limitless, you can make the impossible possible.

Question to innovate

What is the first step to finding the right answer? My response is that asking the right question is essential. For his book *A More Beautiful Question*, American journalist Warren Berger interviewed dozens of companies like Netflix, Google and Airbnb and found that questions are key to innovation and breakthroughs.

The Polaroid camera was created because Edwin Land's daughter asked him, "Why do I have to wait to see the picture?" Airbnb got its start because two flat-mates found themselves wondering why people had to stay in over-priced hotels if they could just get a room in their place to crash.

A questioning culture, he found, ignites both curiosity and creativity, drawing out ideas, solutions and viewpoints that we may have taken for granted or missed. Personally, this is something I have to keep working on. My mentor, Julio Portalatin, has reminded me on a number of occasions that my role as a leader is not to have all the answers, but to ask the right questions. It is always tempting to try and know all the details to determine the answers, but asking the right questions helps to unlock issues, see the same situation from a totally different angle and can result in new, innovative solutions.

I remember applying this when I was starting a new role where the ask was business process transformation. In the early discussions with tenured team members, I heard the following statement many times, "We have always done it this way." We could have employed a team of experts to redesign the business processes and implement them through a change management process that the existing team would likely have resisted.

Instead, we took a slightly more time-consuming approach and sat with the team to ask why things were done this way; what if they were done in another way; and how we could achieve a better process for the customer. The questions were all framed around the objective of improving the customer experience. By engaging the team and asking questions with reference to the customer, it was non-threatening. Ultimately, the team actively participated in helping to redesign an innovative experience for the customer that was most efficient for the business. A win-win for all.

> **TIP #74**
> **The right questions ignite curiosity and creativity, draw out new ideas, solutions and viewpoints that spark innovation.**

Be digitally savvy

We are all acutely aware of how rapidly technology is changing our lives – and that its pace gets faster every year. Companies which are digitally savvy will not just be leaders today but also tomorrow. According to recent research by MIT Sloan, organisations with digitally savvy leaders outperformed peers on revenue growth and valuation by over 48 percent, but only seven percent of large companies report having digitally savvy executive teams[1]. This is something that I often reflect on.

Being digitally savvy is not just about understanding technology. It is also thinking strategically about emerging technologies and how they can drive success in the years ahead. According to MIT Sloan's review of nearly 2,000 companies (many of them non-tech firms), organisations with digitally savvy leaders do a few things differently. They pursue breakthrough performance via innovation, cross-selling and business transformation. They create rapid learning cultures and an environment of constant testing and learning, which allows them to identify and solve problems earlier. Lastly, they coach and communicate, rather than command and control.

Personally, there is always room for me to grow my digital savviness. I like exploring the local tech communities in whichever

---

[1] Weill, Peter et al. "Does Your C-Suite Have Enough Digital Smarts?" *MIT Sloan Management Review*, 3 March 2021, https://sloanreview.mit.edu/article/does-your-c-suite-have-enough-digital-smarts/.

city and country I am living in. Because I relish experiential learning more than formal study, when I have to do the latter, I make it "bite-sized". At home, my family bought me a SkillShare subscription, which I have thoroughly enjoyed. Through it, I learnt more about storytelling and the impact of visual imagery, and explored creative personal interests such as floral arrangement. I make good use of Harvard X and am impressed by many of its courses. I am drawn to the variety of entrepreneurial and intrapreneurial courses available, even for specialist areas such as emerging economies.

> **TIP #75**
> **Being digitally savvy is a commitment to lifelong learning. Digitally savvy leaders must think strategically about emerging technologies and plan for how they can drive success in the years ahead.**

I believe I have much to learn from younger colleagues too. Many of them are digital natives who are comfortable with and fluent in technology. Our workplaces are multi-generational and technology has fundamentally changed the way we communicate and work – and will continue to do so at an incredibly fast pace. It is important for everyone to be open-minded to learn from anyone and everyone so we can harness technology for greater, positive impact.

Unlock intrapreneurship with passion

I once sat in for a discussion with Her Majesty Queen Rania Al Abdullah of Jordan. Some of her thoughts really resonated with me. Specifically, she concluded the discussion reinforcing that we often hold ourselves back: "I am good at x; I am not great at y", and so on. We are confined only by the walls we build in our minds, but we must recognise we have the ability to learn and change.

The event encouraged me to think about design, creation and innovation. While we are no stranger to the Steve Jobs, Jack Mas and Elon Musks of the world, it is a myth that entrepreneurs are the key drivers of innovation in society. The fact is, says Kaihan Krippendorff, innovation expert and author of *Driving Innovation from Within*, over 70 percent of transformative innovations are conceived by intrapreneurs (employees in companies) and without it, there would not be mobile phones, personal computers or email today.

This is due in part, Krippendorff explains, to the advantages intrapreneurs have: scale that entrepreneurs cannot easily match; access to multiple capabilities under one roof; resources their company has to invest and the ability to diversify risks. This excites me because what it means is that each one of us who already works in an organisation has the opportunity to change the world without quitting our jobs!

Unlocking the spirit and power of intrapreneurship takes work. It demands adopting an act-learn-build rather than a prove-plan-execute approach, an environment where disruptive business ideas are born in hallways, not boardrooms and nurturing agile teams, not silos. Winning ideas, Krippendorff says, meet at the crossroads of market need, company need and passion. Passion for seeking out problems and finding solutions; passion for our job and responsibilities, showing care and persistence as though it were our own business; and passion to see each barrier not as a reason to give up but a problem to solve.

TIP #76
Unlock the spirit and power of intrapreneurship by adopting an act-learn-build approach.

I leave you with a fun fact: did you know Steve Wozniak was rejected FIVE times at Hewlett-Packard for his idea, which later became Apple?

Be hard, not harsh

Successful innovation is a lot more than just cultivating a culture where people are free to experiment, to fail, to collaborate and to speak up. All that is important, but as Harvard Professor Gary Pisano shares, it takes equal doses of competence, rigorous discipline to walk away from what does not work, comfort with challenging one another about our ideas, methods and results (what he calls "brutal candour"), a high level of individual accountability and strong leadership[1].

As an organisation shifts into high gear, it needs to get comfortable with innovating for a fast-changing and uncertain future. Being deliberate and disciplined and allocating resources wisely will allow for failing smart and learning even faster. Many organisations struggle to innovate not because they lack good ideas but because they fail to create a supportive environment in which these ideas can flourish.

In an interview, Pisano explains, "There's a difference between being hard and being harsh. Being hard means I'm going to ask

[1] Pisano, Gary. "The Hard Truth About Innovative Cultures." *Harvard Business Review*, Magazine (January–February 2019), https://hbr.org/2019/01/the-hard-truth-about-innovative-cultures.

tough questions; be brutally honest; and hold you accountable for painful decisions such as shutting down projects. Candour is uncomfortable. But it doesn't have to be demeaning. We can create environments where people are counted and treated with respect and dignity. And a number of companies have."

TIP #77

Commit to fostering a culture of innovating for a fast-changing and uncertain future.

Throughout my career as a leader, I have always remained committed to fostering a culture where my team members are empowered to share ideas and innovate. This requires encouraging bold ambitions, being receptive to any ideas and really giving it due consideration. It also requires nurturing a team environment, where there is diversity of thought and debate is welcomed. With them, I share that my hope is that innovation becomes everyone's habit, that they will always strive to do better than the present.

Tap your creative genius

I n 2022, the world celebrated the coolest date of the decade, 22.02.2022. The extremely rare date is both a palindrome and an ambigram as it reads the same from left to right, right to left and upside down. The "Twosday" fell on a Tuesday too – which will not happen for another 400 years in 2422. It was interesting to see the creative ways everyone – from businesses and schools to netizens – marked the occasion. Even Google got in on the act by showering a confetti of twos on screens when you did a "Twosday" search.

Human creativity and our ability to find meaning and connections never ceases to amaze me. And it is growing in importance as automation makes process-driven jobs obsolete and generative AI will surely significantly impact the way we work and live. According to LinkedIn, next to cloud computing, creativity is the second-most in-demand skill in the world. When many of us think of creativity, we think of artists, designers, writers, filmmakers etc. But in reality, all of us have the potential to be creative. Being creative is simply about using our imagination to find new ways of solving challenging situations.

This type of creative thinking is only going to become more in-demand. Just as automation has disrupted production, generative AI will disrupt white-collar, professional roles. Those who refuse to engage will be left behind in some way. The reality is that technology will continue to advance, bringing good and bad, but ignoring it simply is not an option. Intellectual curiosity and creativity could be the key to shaping and harnessing AI to create positive outcomes for jobs, work and life.

International coach and trainer Mark Carter talks about how we can all practice creativity. We can train our brain to always come up with multiple solutions to a problem, switch into "play mode" where we are more comfortable with failure and lastly, disrupt our routines. Practising creativity and changing our brain pathways can happen in small steps, such as taking a new route to work or trying a different coffee. Just disrupting a current routine becomes a form of divergent thinking, opening up possibilities of new ways of thinking.

TIP #78

Creativity is not a role or a hobby. It is a skill we all have and must practise to adapt successfully to change.

For me, meeting new people, learning their stories and beliefs is a form of divergent thinking, that helps me think better and be more open to possibility. I love listening to other people's life stories, their values and beliefs – even if they do not align with my own. Just getting some insight into why people hold their opinions and beliefs is both thought-provoking and impactful and can help me to see that there might be a better way to engage with change.

Embrace a daring vision of the future

Embracing a future-first perspective and being crystal clear about what we want to achieve is more important than ever in an exponentially changing world. This philosophy is beautifully explained by US business consultant Charles E Smith in his paper, "The Merlin Factor: Creating Ambassadors from the future". Though published 25 years ago, it still holds wisdom and value today. Merlin is a reference to the legendary magician in King Arthur's tale, who was said to have been born in the future and aged as he proceeded into the past, influencing events in King Arthur's court by drawing on prescience of their destined outcomes.

In a nutshell, the essence of the Merlin Factor is about a relentless focus on creating a future need and want, and not what we believe we can achieve today. It is about embracing a daring vision of the future that may seem impossible in the now. In his paper, Smith provides examples of NASA's vision to put a man on the moon within the decade some 50 years ago and Caterpillar's bold dream to provide "48 hours parts service anywhere in the world or Cat pays". They may not have had answers to the "how" back then, but their singular focus on achieving their dream and making it a new collective goal across all levels of their organisations helped them turn it into reality.

As Gary Hamel and CK Prahalad wrote in the May-June 1989 issue of the *Harvard Business Review*, "Companies that have risen to global leadership over the past 20 years invariably began with ambitions that were out of all proportion to their resources and capabilities."

TIP #79

Focus on creating a future need, want and ambition, without being limited by what you believe is achievable today.

Having a future-first mindset demands we step out of our current state and forget our current limitations. Recognising that our natural frame of reference is behind us and has no hold on our future is liberating and empowering. As individuals or as organisations, when we look to create a future without artificially imposed limitations, we create opportunities that we might never have dreamed possible.

PROGRESS

LESSONS
I WISHED
I LEARNED
EARLIER ✉

⊛ **McGowan, Renee**
To:

Friday, 14 August 2020 at 9:00 AM

Hi everyone

I hope you had a wonderful week. I had a good week, but frankly it was a bit dull and I felt a bit flat. COVID-19 is taking its toll and I'm grieving all the things that feel (temporarily) lost: face-to-face time with all of you and with our clients; meals out with friends; beach-side vacations and seeing my Mum, Dad and sister.

I know that some of you feel the same with your markets battling a second wave like in the Philippines this week. But I'm also heartened that some of us are experiencing a far more positive outlook locally. I'm buoyed by the better-than-expected economic revival in China and the pace of business activity in Taiwan and South Korea. I'm thrilled to see colleagues being able to meet face-to-face with clients in markets such as Singapore and Thailand. But for those who are feeling the strain of this ultra-marathon, chin up, I'm cheering you on.

There has been nothing typical about this year and it has created a 'collective grief' that is new to many of us. David Kessler is perhaps one of the world's most renowned experts on grief and I've been very interested in his observations. Together with Elizabeth Kubler-Ross, Kessler popularized the well-known five stages of grief: Denial. Anger. Bargaining. Depression. Acceptance. Often referred to as a grief curve, Kessler himself acknowledges that it's important that we recognize these stages of grief are not linear. It doesn't follow timelines or schedules; not everyone goes through all of them or in a prescribed order. He has some great observations on feelings of 'grief' during COVID-19 that I encourage you to read. His thoughts around the 'open-endedness' of the pandemic really resonated with me.

So this week, to support my own wellbeing, I've focused on two things:

1. **What I can control**
· My health and wellbeing – More time at home has helped create new routines. My favorite is an early morning hike with my husband on Friday morning (selfie evidence below! ☺)
· Ensuring our business is strong – I've worked hard this week on the not-so-exciting-but-very-important parts of running our business well. This includes sales pipeline reviews; ensuring invoices are out and then paid promptly; profitability improvements and assessing changes in client demand for our services. This way, I know I'm doing everything I can to ensure that our business is strong and our outlook is bright in spite of global recessionary pressures.

2. **偷得浮生半日闲 (_Tou de fu sheng ban ri xian_)**
I love the sound and meaning of this old Chinese saying. I translate it very loosely to mean 'taking time from your busy schedule to smell the flowers'. This week, I've made sure to steal pockets of time for the things that make me feel good. I sent food and wine treats to my Mum; played a new game with the kids and started doing a puzzle (I don't think I've done a puzzle since I was a child!).

However you're feeling, I encourage you to also focus on what you can control and make time for yourself. Run your client projects/book like it's your own small business; spend time exercising, mediating or relaxing; be generous and compassionate with others as there is 'collective grief in the air'. If you haven't booked annual leave and time off yet, then I urge you to do so. We all need to 'take time'. Also, make use of the resources on our wellness hub Brighter Together.

I can't be with you face-to-face, but I do love connecting. Drop me an email or schedule a virtual coffee chat with me or any of the Asia Leadership Team. I look forward to hearing from you – and don't forget to also share your ideas on Bright Side. I'm counting on you to help us shape a _brighter_ future.

Renee

Fresh from my Fri morning hike

One day 2020 will be the one-word Catch-phrase for everything messed up. "Hows your day?", "A total 2020.", "Say no more."

Post-run with Grace

Treats for my Mum

Start anew anytime

For many of us, the New Year has traditionally been an opportunity to wipe the slate clean, start afresh and embrace new possibilities. It is what behavioural scientist and author of *How to Change: The Science of Getting from Where You Are to Where You want to Be*, D. Katy Milkman, calls "the fresh start effect". In these moments when we can begin anew, we have natural motivation and momentum to make meaningful change and work harder towards our goals.

I think the speed of modern life and the pace of change has challenged this "fresh start effect". The pace at which our lives move makes it more difficult to create distinct "mental accounting periods" or chapters in our lives. I therefore resolve to simply be optimistic and pragmatic at the start of every year. I focus on having a clear picture of where I want to be personally and professionally by the end of that year – healthier, stronger and making a positive impact on our world.

I am also pragmatic in the path to achieving this and recognise that there may be other opportunities during the year to make a fresh start: a new home, job, experience. It may not be easy but as Dr Milkman points out, fresh-start moments are all around us, "You're more likely to step back and think about the big picture of your life during moments that feel like a chapter break in your narrative."

A good piece of advice she gives is to link the change that you want to effect to enjoyment and fun. Need to lose weight? Sign up for dance lessons instead of a gym membership. Research has shown that having fun will motivate you to stay the course for a longer period. "People who pursue their goals in ways that are fun stick to them longer because they aren't fighting an uphill battle," she writes.

TIP #80
There are opportunities to make fresh starts all the time – we just have to be open to them.

It is also beneficial to have a flexible mindset around the fresh start you want to make. If you missed your weekly dance lesson, sign up for something else fun that the studio offers. Dr Milkman calls this an "elastic" approach and says that the antithesis of it, rigidity, is a sure-fire way to kill any enthusiasm towards the change you want to make.

Change your habits; change your life

In a world that shifts rapidly beneath our feet, James Clear, bestselling author of *Atomic Habits*, says our habits can ground us. When we are unsure of what the next day will bring, we return to the fundamentals, to what we can control.

In his book, Clear delves into the surprising power of small habits and how we often focus on our big goals without thinking about the small steps we need to take along the way. Where we want to be is just as important as how we get there – and the small, seemingly insignificant things we do each and every day, add up to meaningful change over time. As Clear puts it beautifully, "habits are the compound interest of self-improvement".

This really struck a chord with me. Often we expect change to happen overnight, lose patience and give up when we do not see results. But in fact, the small habits we build daily – perhaps just carving out 10 minutes to learn something new – compound over time to help us achieve our big goals and ambitions. For me, small habits are both pragmatic and positive. Making sure I exercise every day in some form is a small habit that I can achieve and doesn't carry as much pressure as "60 minutes of cardio exercise, four times per week".

Form habits that help, not hinder

Clear says it all starts with scaling our habits down to something that's simple and takes two minutes or less to do – so we will stick with it. Reading 30 books next year becomes reading a page a day. Exceeding your sales target next year becomes making a phone call to one extra prospect a day. Becoming a better people manager becomes checking in on a colleague every day.

TIP #81

The small, seemingly insignificant things we do each and every day can add up to meaningful change over time.

The daily decisions we make eventually shape our teams, our communities, and ourselves. I truly believe that if we change our habits, we change our lives. When we do one percent more or different each day or week, we'll inculcate patterns of behavior that will in due course help us reach our goals.

Form habits that help, not hinder

The pace of change is faster than ever and the reality is that we have to constantly update our skills and abilities to stay ahead. Conferences and informal learning on the job are all great stepping stones towards achieving our personal and professional growth goals. But to make consistent progress, we need to make learning a habit.

The hardest part is always in taking that first step. Starting small is key, but so is being intentional in making time. Life coach Leo Babauta has good advice on this front, "Make it so easy you can't say no." Expect that there will be regression – but do not beat yourself up over it. Instead, think about why it happened and then quickly get back into it.

An article I once read highlighted that there are no good or bad habits – only effective and ineffective ones. To find out if a habit is helping or hindering you, ask, "Does it help you become the type of person you want to be?" The same article, authored by Dell's James Gibb[1], listed four ways habits can be used to focus on what you want to become:

1. **Create a habits scorecard:** This exercise by James Clear of the book *Atomic Habits* helps to build self-awareness of your behaviour.

---

[1] Gibb, James. "The importance of identity in shaping our habits." *Arabian Business*, 23 August 2022, https://www.arabianbusiness.com/opinion/the-importance-of-identity-in-shaping-our-habits.

2. **Focus on systems over goals:** Goals are important but the process of getting there should not be undermined.

3. **Build keystone habits:** These are the small, low-hanging wins that when achieved, can lead to greater positive change.

4. **Train your willpower muscle:** Yes, it is a muscle that can be strengthened and developed.

I have tried these techniques myself when I once found myself stuck in a rut. I was so busy focused on internal business matters that I was basically oblivious to the world around me – news, current affairs and market trends. While I used to read newspapers, such as *The Economist* and *Foreign Correspondent*, the internal machinations of running a business had crowded out all my time for learning and distanced me from global issues.

Yet, rather than beat myself up over this, I started small, for instance subscribing to daily newspaper summaries like *The Morning* by *The New York Times*. I found a few minutes at the start of the day to read through this to provide me with an overview of the day's events from a US perspective. Over time, I added more of these summary subscriptions from *Bloomberg*,

TIP #82
Create time to make learning a habit. Start small to ensure it does not overwhelm you.

The Economist, The Atlantic and *The Aspen Society*. Before long, I was delving into relevant or interesting information that helped me learn and I had managed to carve out time in the day to do so.

Review your stop-doing list

Too often, we get caught up with productivity – how can I do more in a set amount of time? But I think the better question really should be "how can I create better outcomes with the resources I have?" Rather than look at the length of the to-do list and figure out how long it will take to clear it, we need to decide what on the list is necessary and worth doing in the limited time that we have. And this calls for ruthless prioritisation, as Sheryl Sandberg puts it[1].

This is something I wished I had learnt earlier in my career. As my career progressed and I took on larger and broader roles, I found myself doing more and more. It took some time (and a few failures) to realise that you cannot just keep doing more when given a bigger job or if the environment or business changes around you.

Starting a new role requires you to reflect on the responsibilities and deliverables of the role, what is required to be done and how you will prioritise activities to achieve the deliverables. Rarely can you operate in a new role in exactly the same way as you have in the past. What has got you here, will not get you where you need to go next.

---

[1] Bariso, Justin. "Sheryl Sandberg Just Gave Some Brilliant Career Advice. Here It Is in 2 WordsIt's time to leave the good behind, and start focusing on the great." *Inc.*, 19 June 2020, https://www.inc.com/justin-bariso/sheryl-sandberg-just-gave-some-brilliant-career-ad.html.

Similarly, when the economic environment changes – for example when a market downturn occurs – your business might need to reduce its expenses and resources to sustain through the slowdown. You cannot keep doing exactly the same activities. It requires reassessment of what is essential to be delivered and then to make the tough decisions about what to stop.

Not ruthlessly prioritising is a failure of leadership as it is inevitably setting a team up to fail. By doing so, it helps a team or entire business be clear on what is important and fundamental to deliver. It gives a team permission to say no to the nice-to-haves, even as they align on what needs to be done. I therefore always encourage others to think about outcomes and the "stop-doing" list.

TIP #83

Don't just focus on what you need to do; think about what you need to stop doing too.

As much as we focus on what needs to get done, we need to know what we need to *stop doing* to make it happen. We can all start by asking ourselves, "Is this really important? Does this help our team achieve our goals? What impact would this make?"

Ask and you shall receive

No matter how strong I think I am, I am only human with both strengths and weaknesses. As such, I have accepted that it is okay to be vulnerable and ask for help. As executive coach Peter Bregman puts it, "Our struggles do not define us any more than our successes do. You are not weak; you have weaknesses. There is a difference."

When you do ask for help, you will find quickly enough that people are very generous in rendering it. In fact, research shows that we regularly underestimate people's willingness to help. Whether seeking support on a difficult client proposal or more resources for our team, it can feel uncomfortable to approach others for help. We may not want to appear weak or selfish, or we assume no one can help us; but if others do not know what we need, they cannot help us. Unfortunately, singularly shouldering everything can lead to burnout.

As a leader, it is even tougher to ask for help. I was diagnosed with thyroid cancer in 2022. Fortunately, it was detected early and is a type of cancer that is relatively easy to treat with surgery and sometimes, radiation. For me, the diagnosis came out of the blue and was not particularly troubling – more inconvenient.

I had one surgery and was back at work within the week and was not missed any more than if I had been on vacation. When a second surgery was required, I took the same approach and despite repeated offers from my team, I leant only on a couple of them for the minimum amount of help I thought to ask for.

In hindsight, I realised mine was not the right approach. My absence had been more noticeable and being unwilling to ask for help had been detrimental to my recovery, making it slower. My team also fed back to me their disappointment towards how I did not care enough for myself – they said I should have asked more for their help.

My experience is an extreme example – it is not always an illness or significant event that precipitates the need to ask for help. Sometimes, we might just be overwhelmed with the volume of work or a specific problem, or we might be struggling with a relationship with a colleague or stakeholder. There are many, many instances where we need to ask for help.

TIP #84

It is okay to ask for help and to do it often. Just be clear about it and seek it from the right people.

What is the best way to ask for help then? I found a podcast by Professor Wayne Baker particularly useful[1]. He shares some good strategies, including being clear about your goals and why you need the help, as well as communicating the request (note that it should direct the other party to be able to take action) in a specific and meaningful manner. Another good tip: asking the right people for help. Says Baker, "It may be better to give than to receive, but it's best to give and to receive."

[1] Beard, Alison, host. "The Art of Asking for (and Getting) Help." *HBR IdeaCast*, episode 714 Harvard Business Review, 17 December 2019, https://hbr.org/podcast/2019/12/the-art-of-asking-for-and-getting-help.

Treat feedback as a gift

Receiving feedback can be an uncomfortable process, especially when it is not complimentary. Still, it is important to heed it and something that I take seriously. At Marsh McLennan, we conduct regular employee surveys to get input from our colleagues. It is always heartening to hear that they feel welcomed, empowered to share new ideas and challenge the status quo, and more importantly feel cared for and supported by the firm. I also make it a point to convey my gratitude for feedback on areas that we need to do better in – usually in areas such as supporting well-being, recognising performance and providing more visibility around internal career opportunities.

I think feedback is a gift. It helps us see our blind spots and, as inspirational speaker Simon Sinek puts it, tells us how we can improve if we do not know how to. Rather than take offense at it or be defensive, it is important to keep an open mind and realise that the giver of the feedback is demonstrating care. No one is going to bother with telling you how to be a better version of yourself if they do not care about you.

In an article for *Inc.*, Jim Schleckser, who leads The CEO Project, offered five rules that he uses to encourage feedback:

1. **Always say "yes, please" when someone asks to give you feedback.** Do not miss the opportunity to collect feedback on your actions and behaviours.

2. **Listen intently.** If someone is willing to give you feedback, do not interrupt them.
3. **If you do not understand the feedback, ask questions until you truly understand what the person is trying to tell you.** This is about seeking to understand.
4. **Maintain an open attitude.** No matter how harsh the feedback might seem, it is a valuable piece of data.
5. **Always thank the person for giving you feedback.** This is a form of feedback to the giver too and hopefully will result in behaviour that others will follow.

I would add to the above list a sixth rule, which is to avoid being immediately defensive. Even if we know the feedback is coming from a place of good intentions, it is almost human nature to defend ourselves. Avoid doing this and instead, pause, listen and reflect. You may want to provide some further context or an explanation, but it is better to do that later, after you have reflected and thought through the feedback and how it may help you.

TIP #85

Do not shy away from receiving constructive feedback from anyone, even if it is not complimentary.

Start small to build big

Much has been written about how big changes start with small actions. Micro habits are what help us conquer big goals. These could be as simple as deliberately doing small acts of kindness – a smile, a handwritten card to show appreciation, buying someone a coffee – which can make a big difference in someone's day and life.

As a business leader, I make it a point to keep my "door always open" to anyone who wants to talk about an issue or idea. I regularly have colleagues drop by, chat in the pantry or send me an email, and we do not just talk about work. We talk about our lives, family and often career or personal challenges. I also reach out to new starters when they join the organisation.

Obviously, I cannot meet everyone, but from the feedback I have received, inviting a colleague out for a coffee to learn about where they have come from and their life and work experiences helps set a tone that ours is a non-hierarchical, inclusive and open workplace that they can be proud of. This is the type of organisation I strive to create.

As Bill Taylor, co-founder of *Fast Company* puts it beautifully, our small gestures send big signals about who we are, what we care about and why we do what we do[1]. He is absolutely right.

TIP #86

Small, positive gestures can create a culture that conquers big goals.

---

[1] Taylor, Bill. "Great Leaders Understand Why Small Gestures Matter." *Harvard Business Review*, 13 January 2020, https://hbr.org/2020/01/great-leaders-understand-why-small-gestures-matter.

Do not underestimate face-to-face time

Nothing replaces face-to-face contact when it comes to building enduring relationships whether with clients or colleagues. Research backs this. Face-to-face meetings build an emotional connection and loyalty, which in turn makes it 71 percent more likely for a client to recommend a brand or company.

A study by Associate Professor Vanessa Bohns[1], who teaches Organizational Psychology at Cornell University, found that a face-to-face request is 34 times more successful than an email, stating that we often underestimate the power of our persuasiveness when we communicate face-to-face. So the next time you need to send an email containing a request, pause and ask if it can be done in person.

The advantages are numerous. In addition to developing a human connection, it makes communication clearer. Assuming you have clearly articulated your query, you can immediately get feedback from the other person through the non-verbal cues. Additionally, you will not have to fret about a long response time or grapple with technology hiccups.

I am acutely reminded of the power of face-to-face time

---

[1] Bohns, Vanessa. "A Face-to-Face Request Is 34 Times More Successful Than an Email." *Harvard Business Review*, 11 April 2017, https://hbr.org/2017/04/a-face-to-face-request-is-34-times-more-successful-than-an-email.

whenever I start a new role. In a global leadership role, it is not possible to immediately meet in-person with a new team or all clients, and so initial interactions are often virtual. These are always helpful for understanding the business, the team or clients' issues and for general knowledge exchange.

However, the strength of the relationship and true connectivity is enhanced enormously when face-to-face. When I am able to visit a new team member or client, we can sit together and talk through business issues. Our interaction is richer, deeper, more impactful and usually results in a better outcome. Then, when we can take that further and connect over a meal as people, we can establish a meaningful connection through our shared experiences of family and personal interests. Over time we can establish trust, a critical ingredient for any successful relationship.

TIP #87

When possible, opt for the in-person meeting, as it helps to develop a human connection and makes communication clearer.

Ultimately, what I have learned is that the best client experience stems from how they were made to feel. Clients appreciate when their partners own the problem, show empathy, personalise their approach and so on. Nowhere is this more palpable than when done in person.

偷得浮生半日闲

tōu   dé   fú   shēng   bàn   rì   xián

ronically, the human race is living longer than ever before, but we seem to be in a much bigger rush and constantly short of time. The pace at which we choose to live and work creates a hurriedness that makes us task orientated, with constant lists and things that need to be done. We compare ourselves to others and, increasingly, the fragmented and unrealistic versions of life published through social media.

It certainly does not help that the world is turbulent, full of change, in almost constant upheaval and organised by 24/7 news cycles that perpetuate more negativity than optimism for the future.

No wonder than that it is very easy to be overwhelmed. We see evidence of this in unprecedented levels of human anxiety and the increased need for preventive mental wellbeing.

No one is immune – me included. Through tough times, dark days and many experiences, I have found two things what works for me. I share these as my final tip, in the hope that they may be helpful for you:

1. **Focus on what you can control**

   Polycrisis, permacrisis…there will be an endless number of things in our life that we cannot control. Over-focusing on them and letting them absorb your thinking and impact your decision-making (or lack of it) serves no positive purpose. For me, I focus on the things I can control – my health and wellbeing and that of my family, how I show up every day committed to do my best and the kindness I can give for free. Focusing more on what you can control and less on what you cannot creates a cycle of positivity and an optimism that can be infectious. It is what works for me.

TIP #88
Focus on what you can control and take time to stop and smell the roses.

2. **偷得浮生半日闲** (*tōu dé fú shēng bàn rì xián*)
I love the meaning of this Chinese saying, which means "stealing half a day's worth of time to spend on leisure".

The English equivalent is to stop and smell the roses. I have learnt to do this regularly. It helps me celebrate great moments, take joy in daily small moments and express gratitude and appreciation for all that I have and can give.

8 TIPS FOR WOMEN LEADERS ✉

t would be remiss of me not to acknowledge the extra hurdles that women leaders have and continue to endure. The representation of women at the most senior levels of government, organisations and boards is still disappointingly low and progress is slow. We must do better and proactively create the equity necessary to ensure everyone thrives.

These eight final tips are relevant for all leaders, but from my experience, are highlights for women as they progress in their careers.

1. **Know your edge as a woman: You are more empathic**

   In general, women can think more broadly yet be empathic, an important leadership trait. This is what it boiled down to in a study published in the *Harvard Business Review*[1] that said that women who lead in times of crisis outperform their male counterparts.

2. **Make resilience your best friend**

   It is so confronting to be a woman leader that you have to be resilient if you want to keep at it. I have heard stories about my male counterparts laying bets on how long I would last in a new leadership position. I still routinely have to tolerate being the only female in meetings, and attending business dinners where the female administrative assistants are invited, so I am not the only woman present. If I was not strong in the face of all these, I would have given up long ago.

---

[1] Zenger, Jack and Joseph Folkman. "Research: Women Are Better Leaders During a Crisis." *Harvard Business Review*, 30 December 2020, https://hbr.org/2020/12/research-women-are-better-leaders-during-a-crisis.

3. **Create your own *modus operandi***

   In local or global roles, there are some uncomfortable realities you cannot escape. While working in Asia, I had to find a way to deal with the drinking culture in Korea and Japan, which was not for me. I ended up developing my own mechanisms – just as you should. For instance, I always had "a call with the team from New York at 10pm" and would need to be back in my hotel room just before that. It takes planning to figure out what works best for you and confidently put it into action.

4. **Be mindful that you are in a position to be a change-maker**

   As you get to senior positions, in most environments, as a woman, you are still a minority. But you are also in a position of power to be a role model by effecting change and ensuring that more women are getting a seat at your table. From your leadership position, you can effect this change in individual instances, but also systemically, forcing the organisation to deliver more equity, pay equality and opportunity for all.

5. **Define what success looks like**

   Everyone wants to be successful but that means different things to different people – and may mean different ways of working. Figure out what it means to you, within the context of your organisation and the stakeholders that surround you. Shift the focus to outputs, rather than inputs. Get really granular, qualify and quantify outputs, revisit them via demonstrable milestones. Then, when it is time to do a performance review, the results and value will speak for themselves. Repeat this every year.

6. **Direct is the way to go**

You are paving your own path. No one else can do it for you. Be clear about what you want and have the confidence to have direct conversations about where you want to go and how. If you leave space for ambiguity, chances are you will leave others (from your managers to your direct reports and peers) confused and uncertain. Respectful, direct and open discussions, and subsequent clarity, works better for everyone.

7. **Mentor and network**

You will need mentors, and you will need to provide mentorship. Start a formal programme in your organisation, if there is not already one. Do it informally too. You will be surprised by how many leaders or people you admire will be open to a supportive discussion and can then refer you to others also. This may result in formal mentorship or an expanded network of diverse people, and you can draw from their strength and experiences, just as they do yours.

8. **Express gratitude**

Even as you are pushing your team for the best results and performance numbers, never forget that they are on their own path too. You can help everyone stay aligned by acknowledging this and saying thank you, especially when they have done their job and done it well. It goes so far in boosting someone's confidence.

If I Could Only Tell You ONE Thing

Create your own path.

Throughout your life and career, you are going to read, learn, experience and receive a lot of advice. Some learnings will be incidental, others will be hugely impactful. Some will be irrelevant and if you are lucky, some will be life-changing. You will have many opportunities to observe successful people and for many of them, you will admire and wonder what the secret to their success is.

My view is that the secret to *your* success lies within you. Only you can decide your purpose, your goals and how you will work to shape the career and life that you want. I hope that the tips in this book have fuelled and inspired your thinking and planning, but if I could only tell you ONE thing, it would be to create your own path.

Be curious, bold and a lifelong learner. Chart your own course both in life and as a leader. The road is unlikely to be linear and you will need to adjust and change along the way as you grow, but there is only one person who knows best how to ensure your success – and that is YOU.

More About This Work In Progress

"I always wanted to run businesses"

The closing tip I shared in the previous page was to create your own path. This is advice that I wish I had earlier in my life and career, when I too often compared myself to others or tried to make somebody else's path work for me.

It is a common misconception, one that says careers are planned methodically, with each rung of the proverbial ladder clearly defined. I certainly did not start my career with specific goals, a well-laid plan or even a desire to lead others. In fact, my progression into senior leadership was not a straight upward climb. While not terribly dramatic, there were many ups and downs, twists and turns, including working part-time for eight years to take care of my three children while they were young.

What I did know was that from a young age, I always wanted to run businesses. Mum recalls the story of a family holiday to Sydney when I was less than 10 years old: while the Sydney Opera House was interesting, it was the "suits" on George Street hurrying to and from meetings that I ogled at. Four decades later, I continue to remain besotted by the structure and dynamics of businesses and the challenge of growing within a larger organisation that has competing priorities.

This explains why I graduated from Monash University with a double degree in Commerce and Arts and, at best, a broad plan to work in a professional, corporate environment. The only slightly longer-term aspiration was for the exotic lights of Asia to shine in my eyes. In my final year, I had offers from various corporate graduate programs and chose a renowned Australian bank, Colonial Bank, that offered to accelerate my long-term ambition by actually including a placement in Asia, where it had a strong presence.

Unfortunately, this was in 1997 and as I finished my final study year, the Asian financial crisis scuppered my Asia placement and I was re-directed to a boutique pension and investment consulting business owned by the bank. I did not realise it then, but this was my first lesson about the need to be open to new and unexpected experiences.

Embracing the consulting environment and keenly observing and learning from experienced consultants helped me pick up on how to understand the business issues of clients and then advise on change. I was inspired by the grey-haired expertise of many of my (mostly male) colleagues, but also the incredible dynamism of the under-30-year-old female leader who ran the business, Annette King.

She was assigned by the bank as my official mentor under the graduate program. I still remember our first meeting over lunch, where she peppered me with questions and indirectly challenged me to consider channelling my ambition more purposefully – what path did I want to not just follow, but create?

Thus began a mentorship and friendship that has lasted close to three decades and has shaped, guided and inspired my career. Mentorship moved to sponsorship, as she created opportunities for me to join her in one of her senior leadership roles. You could say my early career was characterised by diverse experiences, varied learning and ongoing encouragement, mentoring and sponsorship from great leaders around me.

In 2001, I joined Mercer, one of four businesses that is today part of Marsh McLennan. Working as a junior consultant alongside incredibly intelligent actuaries and investment professionals taught me the value that consultants can provide to clients and the impact this has not just on an organisation, but also on the individual lives of its employees. It reminded me that I am not naturally skilled at either math or spreadsheets, resulting in many weekends of (often frustrating) self-learning of both statistics and Microsoft Excel.

Three years later, I moved on to product and marketing functions where I learnt, through practice, the importance of understanding your audience, assessing market demand, testing and iterating, having relevant messages and a clear (measurable) call to action. It reinforced that I have a strong creative side and that designing, writing, colour and imagery was personally energising (and ironically made the spreadsheets a bit easier to manage – perhaps the right brain providing some relief to the left side!).

Working with the sales team was inevitable and that taught me the art and science of selling. Great sales producers showed me the methodical approach to building relationships, truly understanding the needs of an organisation and focusing on the client, instead of how great the organisation I work for is. I learnt that I thrive in a high-energy environment, but that eating candy non-stop, while pulling an "all-nighter" for a proposal submission, is not a good idea.

As my career progressed, my roles naturally became more demanding and, as I have come to learn, more impactful – and dependent – on those around me. In 2013, I took on my first C-suite position as the Chief Customer & Marketing Officer of Mercer Australia. I have not turned back since, growing into various leadership roles that were offered, where I had to rapidly learn that the measure of my success was how I could create, nurture and support a high-performing team to succeed. This came full circle when I realised that my success was largely due to those who have nurtured and supported me.

"I spend the first three months saying I can't do it"

This might come as a surprise and is probably a trait more often attributed to men than women; but throughout my career, I have frequently voluntarily put up my hand for a new project or role. Rarely was I "qualified", according to a formal job description or list of skills, experiences and requirements.

However, I did not "fake it till I make it"; I was honest in my ambition and made a commitment to try, learn and seek guidance when needed. I asked that it was a two-way relationship – requesting my manager or team to proactively tell me if they thought I was heading off-course. Many of these experiences, and the leaders who took a chance on me in early career roles (or got tired of my pushing or nagging), have, years later, sponsored my career through senior leadership roles.

I will confess that even as I put up my hand, self-doubt lingered. My husband, Nick Labans, will tell you that I spend the first three months in every new role telling him I cannot do it. In the early part of my career, it was weighted more to what I personally did (or did not) know to be successful in the role. I would frequently say to Nick, "I'm not ready for this, it's too hard."

At the same time, it never occurred to me to not continue. I would just make small plans: this week I will focus on meeting these new people, next week I will focus on understanding this business issue that is prevailing. I would typically work in a three-month-plan format, where each month had a clear set of deliverables. It was the methodical way I could keep working through and focusing on learning everything I had to in order to be successful in the role.

As my career progressed, the self-doubt leaned more to whether I could shape the role and the organisational direction successfully. Absorbing enough data, insights and information was important, but making sure that I had the right leadership team and that the business had diverse skills, capabilities and strong talent became critical. Macro-economic, geo-political, competitor and external trends featured more and added to self-doubt as they impacted the role and business significantly – but were all out of my control.

I learnt to take the same approach: to break down the milestone deliverables, get feedback and alignment from stakeholders and then focus on delivering these. Over time, with growing knowledge, evidence of successful deliverables and expanded networks, I was able to move beyond self-doubt and the short-term plan, and focus on a longer-term vision and strategy.

I now think that EVERYONE taking on a new role should feel some nervousness and apprehension. I use this as a sign that this is the right role for them – it has stretch and development opportunity. Conversely, if someone is 100 percent confident going into a role, it is probably not the right role for them and may be short-lived.

"My mentors are an invaluable part of my leadership journey"

I have been blessed to work with a number of talented and inspiring leaders who took me under their wing to challenge, push and accelerate my learning and success. With the exception of my first mentor who was assigned (poor Annette King did not know at the time it would be a lifelong assignment!), I met most of them through putting up my hand or leaning into a challenging opportunity.

An early customer relationship management project sparked an unofficial mentorship under senior Mercer Executive David Anderson and then sponsorship to take on a role leading the creation of a retail marketing function. For the next 20 years, he pushed and prodded me, encouraging me to assume roles that I may not have been fully ready for but believing I could do them. He did not cut me any slack, had high expectations and was clear with me when I was meeting them and when I was not. When it was the latter, he coached me through to learn more and be better.

One CEO in particular, Ben Walsh, without knowing me well, took a gamble to involve me in his office. Thus began a part-time, chief-of-staff type role that put me on a leadership path after some years of part-time work and time at home with my children. He coached me through learning how to engage more effectively with diverse, global stakeholders, board members and regulatory bodies. He challenged me to consider local strategy in a global context, thus expanding the capabilities necessary to lead in a global organisation. Then, when the opportunity arose, he supported my growth into a senior leadership role responsible for the delivery of customer services to our then more than one million retail investors.

Another CEO who supported me was Julio Portalatin. When we met, he was Mercer's global CEO and was visiting Australia as part of a round-the-world check-in. Unfortunately my team was scheduled to meet him on the last slot of his first day in Melbourne. I knew immediately that I had to do something different than death-by-PowerPoint. Sitting him down in yet another meeting room at 5pm and delivering a presentation to him after he had arrived that morning from New York City was surely a *kamikaze* mission.

Instead, to introduce the amazing customer service team I was then leading, we hosted a standing cocktail event with an interactive quiz and game. Through an engaging way, we demonstrated the diverse skills and capabilities that enabled us to successfully help over 3,500 daily customer transactions through our digital platforms, call centre and advisory centres.

This sparked a formal mentor relationship and then sponsorship that was life-changing. I was pushed and challenged more than ever before, but also given access to many different leaders that I would not normally have had the chance to interact with. Over time and with more experience and connectivity globally, I was encouraged to apply for a senior leadership position overseas. I was not successful the first time, but later, the right opportunity presented itself. It was with much enthusiasm that my family and I embarked on a new chapter by moving first to New York, and then later, Hong Kong and in 2022, Dubai.

I cannot talk about the positions in the latter two cities without mentioning yet another mentor, this time Martine Ferland, the first non-American global CEO of Mercer. Working with her has been a privilege. Her sponsorship elevated me to the Global Executive Leadership team for the first time and exposed me to the greatest challenges of my career. It also gave me the most incredible opportunity to observe her unique leadership style that combines economics, empathy and humanity.

To date (2023), I have worked with Mercer and Marsh McLennan for over 20 years. One of the reasons for this is that the culture creates and attracts great leaders, who in turn lead businesses that provide extraordinary opportunities for their people and then actively support their success.

Certainly, there have also been many opportunities to consider other organisations and roles. By happy coincidence, each time this occurred, a new internal role would emerge to offer me new learning points, challenges and the chance to work with diverse, intelligent and kind people, often in different countries. That is how the last two decades have flown by (though the speed does horrify me!). During that time, I have worked in over 10 different roles, lived in five very diverse countries and collaborated with world-leading organisations and institutions and some of the brightest advisers in the world. It has been a great career so far.

"I was ready to drop out of school by 15"

My story would be incomplete without delving into some detail about my roots. I was born into a middle-class family in Melbourne, Australia in the 1970s and am not abashed to say I have always wanted to make some money – not because we lacked anything in life or in our family, but rather that I saw having sufficient income and savings seemed to offer more choices in life. If you live pay cheque to pay cheque, your paths can be limited.

I was always rebellious too. I never slept as a baby and neither of my parents are sure how they overcame that to have a second child, my sister. They still seem traumatised by their experience as new parents.

The first time they knew that trouble was going to be my middle name was when I was about 18 months old. I had sat myself beside a potted plant and decided it was fun to take the dirt out and put it on the floor. When Mum saw it, she told me "no" and immediately

Growing up carefree in suburban Australia.

moved me away to do something else. Apparently, I was not having any of it and went right back to the potted plant. This went on for a full day and I did not stop or tire, much less eat or sleep. When Dad came home from work, that is how he found us. Knowing the circumstances, I may have stayed by the plant until I finally fell asleep.

As an early teen, I refused to conform to fashion and trends, preferring instead to be doing or wearing something "creative". While my parents were adamant about me not having body piercings, Mum did permit the use of my hair as a way of self-expression. You can imagine my delight upon learning this. From a shaved head to coloured and spiked hair, I have sported them all. Dad, till this day, still speaks with mild horror about the time I came home with a large peace symbol shaved on the back of my head. All I can say now is thank goodness this was pre-social media!

My yearning to make some money led me to offer washing windows as a service as a teenager. In Victoria, the legal age for being employed then was 14 years nine months. I, of course, had no intention of waiting until then. I figured if I was not "employed" by somebody else, I could still work and earn my own money.

That is how I found myself washing windows at 12 or 13 years old, during the summer and throughout the school holidays. I remember making a good amount of money, albeit more from the generosity of local shopkeepers trying to encourage me than the quality of my window washing skills. Yet, it was very satisfying work, being physical (and hot during the Australian summer), so I felt like I really earned it.

Over time, I expanded my services to more shops and had a friend join me. I was very proud to have generated some income when everyone had said I was not old enough to work. I guess in

As an exchange student in Indonesia and my wonderful Indonesian family.

today's language, this made me entrepreneurial, but in the 1980s, I just wanted to work and earn money during my school holidays.

Strangely, my conscientious streak did not permeate my student life. While I went to a good local primary school, I could not say the same about high school. By the age of 15, I was so bored I was ready to drop out. I could have gone down that path but for some reason, I did not. I applied for an exchange programme to Germany and a scholarship for a private school, St Margaret's, that my parents had always wanted me to go to but could not afford. I got accepted by both but ended up choosing the latter.

This was a turning point and probably the only reason that I did not drop out of school. I appreciated the privilege I was offered every day, where I literally would have to walk up the steep driveway to school. Despite the effort, it was flanked by the most beautiful gardens with a panoramic view of the school fields and faculty buildings – I considered it a daily moment of gratitude.

When I graduated, I signed myself up for another exchange programme, this time to Indonesia. Since I had to fund it myself, I opted to experience life in our closest neighbour as it was also very different from Australia. It turned out to be a formative experience because I lived with a local family, headed by their father, Kusfandi, and went to a nearby art school.

Although I could rotate among different families, I ended up staying with only this one. It allowed me to develop close relationships with two of Kusfandi's three daughters, Retno and Titi, who were still living at home then. Retno was studying her MBA and Titi, art. Being wonderfully different, they exposed me to different worlds and social circles. Till today, I continue to love them and regard them as my sisters. Throughout university, I would visit them or they would come over and we spent about 10 years moving in and out of each other's houses and lives. Naturally, I became fluent in Bahasa Indonesia.

I entered university in 1994 and although it was in the same city as where my family and I were living, I made the decision – a silly one in hindsight – to move out of home. I did not realise how expensive renting was but I was too stubborn and proud to change my mind. This meant I had to scrimp and save throughout the four years, working part-time to earn enough for food and board.

One of my jobs was at a gas station in a combined industrial and residential area, where I spent three half-days a week during the school term behind the cash register from 3pm to midnight. I did not realise it then, but this was where I had the first opportunity to learn about how to anticipate and deliver customer needs, and also have some fun at work.

Around 10pm every night, some workers from a nearby factory would come in while on their shift break. They were always in a rush as presumably, they only had a short break. I quickly realised the same few people were coming in and buying the same types of snacks – so I would have them bagged and ready when they came in. Not only did this surprise them at first, it also made them happy. We would have a chat and I like to think it made both our evenings a little less dull.

Over time, more workers came to buy snacks. There were a lot of variances, but a Coca-Cola, Mars bar and packet of cigarettes were the most common. Before long, I had a 10pm "rush-hour", where I would have many bags lined up and ready to ring up. The number of interactions grew and I had some good laughs with them. I was surprised to learn how much people appreciated it when someone was familiar with their order – it brought a sense of belonging and loyalty.

I learnt to do this also at other times during my shift, when I would have a customer's favourite snack or brand of cigarettes ready to go on the counter. Unconsciously, I was learning so many things through this experience: engaging with diverse people, building relationships, customer experience and sales. Having to work through university exposed me to a whole other world of learning beyond what I was being taught at school.

When I graduated from Monash University, I stopped working at the gas station but till this day, continue to carry those lessons with me. Naturally, I have added many more but still cannot help but feel I have barely scratched the surface, hence the notion of "work in progress". That said, whatever I have learnt so far is embedded in this book and I hope it will become a trusty companion in your journey.

Acknowledgements

Thank you...

Mum and Dad, for the sacrifices you made to provide an education that changed my life. And for always believing that there are no limits to what Sheena and I can achieve.

Natalie Truong, for always pushing me to be better, to be bolder, to meet new people and to try something new – and to laugh! Your selflessness, creativity and positivity makes everyone around you one percent better and makes the world better, stronger and happier.

Irene Kew for being a gifted colleague, great friend and adviser. Despite oceans between us (literally), our minds are connected and you tirelessly improved the way I think, engage and write. You helped create a community among and of thousands during a time when everyone was distanced, isolated and despairing. You found the light for us and helped me shine the light to touch our colleagues in our Friday emails. Without you, this book wouldn't have been possible. My wonderful creative friends Amy Quigley and Kathleen Van Nest Pierce for your encouragement and input to everything from fonts to title. And to Darcy McGirr, without your organisation skills I simply wouldn't have had time to complete the book!

Shi Ping for your patience, editing and friendship. You helped me unpack my own story, listened and wade through hundreds of Friday emails to distill the leadership tips. Just as Natalie taught us, trying something new opens us to new experiences, learning and friendship. I know ours will endure – I hope to book #2.

Printed in the USA
CPSIA information can be obtained
at www.ICGtesting.com
LVHW030828301023
762155LV00002B/2

9 789811 284663